# The Golf Gods

## Who They Are, What They Want & How to Appease Them

### Robert Brown

Illustrations by Roger Schillerstrom

SMG
SPORTS
MEDIA
GROUP

SPORTS
MEDIA
GROUP®

Text Copyright © 2007 Robert A. Brown
Illustrations Copyright © 2007 Roger Schillerstrom

All inquiries should be addressed to:
Sports Media Group
An imprint of Ann Arbor Media Group
2500 S. State Street
Ann Arbor, MI 48104

Printed in the United States of America.

1 2 3 4 5

Library of Congress Cataloging in Publication data

Brown, Robert A. (Robert Alexander), 1946–
The golf gods : who they are, what they want, and how to appease them / Robert Brown ; illustrations by Roger Schillerstrom.
p. cm.
ISBN-13: 978-1-58726-451-1 (hardcover : alk. paper)
ISBN-10: 1-58726-451-X (hardcover : alk. paper)
1. Golf—Humor. 2. Gods—Humor. I. Title.

PN6231.G68B76 2007
818'.602—dc22

2007003240

# Other Golf Books
# by Robert Brown

*A Thousand Rounds of Golf: Over a Half Century of Tips from Pros, Top Amateurs, and Weekend Phenomenons*

*The Golfing Mind: The Psychological Principles of Good Golf*

*The Way of Golf: Reconnecting with the Soul of the Game*

*To Deena,*
*who gave me her hand in the*
*Scottish town of Dornoch*

# Contents

# The First Word

If you play golf you know that one minute the game can fill you with pride, and seconds later your heart is ripped out of your chest. You have rejoiced at a blast from the sand that bounces twice and rolls into the cup. You have suffered when you left a seventy-five-foot eagle chip one roll short. If you thought about it, you might realize you have suffered more than you rejoiced. You begin play with the best of intentions and in the best of moods, yet often end up miserable somewhere on the back nine and often enough begin the downward spiral by the third hole. But you persevere and return for more. Is golf cursed? Are you cursed? What is the meaning of it all? How can golf include all the joys and sorrows of life in one game, sometimes in one shot? These pages will explain this mystery.

Much of the answer lies in the dark shadows of the human psyche. Some of it lies in the inherent unfairness of the game. A large portion lies within what some believe is the purview of the golf gods. You may have read about them in such reputable magazines as *Sports Illustrated*. Regarding the difficult playing conditions of the 2006 U.S. Open at Winged Foot, *SI* said simply, "the golf gods were playing rough." You hear mention of them on television; "The golf gods sure helped on that shot, Bobby." "They sure did, Billy." Your friends make comments. You may have said some things about them yourself. This book was written to help you get to know the golf gods, to understand them, and to learn how to make them your friends.

All the facts presented here are true. Everything else is also true to varying degrees. There is no guarantee that what you learn will help you. There can never be such a guarantee. The golf gods are, after all, more knowledgeable, more powerful, more insightful, and more aware than all the golfers in the world put together. But they genuinely care about you. That makes all the difference. They know how difficult golf is and want to help you play your best and enjoy yourself more than ever before. You deserve nothing less.

Living in the modern world isn't easy. There are deadlines, bills, diets, crowds, taxes, expiration dates—you name it, we have to deal with it. To put things in perspective, imagine how difficult life was three thousand years ago. The ancient Greeks had to start understanding the world pretty much from scratch and didn't always know what they were doing. Zeno of Elea, for example, who lived about 450 B.C., argued that getting from one place to another was impossible. He postulated that if an arrow flew from the bow to the target, say, from point A to point B, it could never arrive. The idea is that before the arrow reaches point B it has to travel through a spot between A and B, say A-1. Then it has to pass through another point, A-2 then A-3 then A-4, and so on. You could slice the distance into an infinite number of pieces. Thus, an arrow would have to pass though a never-ending number of points between A and B and therefore would never make it to B, the target. Ergo, going from point A to point B is impossible. Don't blame me. This is how they thought in those days.

Luckily, the ancient Greeks produced a lot of top cogitators like Euclid, Pythagoras, Archimedes, Hippocrates, Plato, and Socrates. These were the big hitters of the era. But what Greece had going for it more than anything else were exactly 3,676 gods, goddesses, and other mythical figures. Beginning with Chaos, a primal force and the great-great-grandparent of Zeus, the Greeks had just about every life event handled by one god or another. Got a problem? Sacrifice the right thing to the right god and you're on your way. The ancient Greeks did all right.

We golfers can do all right too, for in the microcosm of life that is golf we are fortunate to have twenty-three golf gods. That is plenty for now. They are able to vastly increase any golfer's enjoyment of the game if that golfer is willing to accept their help. At the moment, not many do. The majority of golfers, for example, buy a new driver without seeking advice from one of the golf gods. Many accept the congratulations of fellow players after a good shot without the merest mention of thanks to a golf deity. How many tour pros mention the golf gods publicly after winning a tournament and a million dollars? None,

that's how many. Zip. Nada. All this can change, now, with you.
Read this book for your pleasure and the benefit of your game.
The wisdom herein is an elixir for any malady, the answer for
any question, the joy of a high draw rather than a weak fade.
Ignore its lessons and there will be consequences. The choice is
yours. Keep in mind, though, the choice the golf gods want you
to make.

# In the Beginning, Now, and the Hereafter

Most golfers at one time or other have called out to the golf gods, usually with an anguished wail as a ball is about to fly into trouble. Sometimes, though rarely, it's a shout of delighted surprise. Always, the golfer has swung, and something has happened seemingly outside the golfer's control and thus in the realm of the gods. The trouble is the great majority of golfers who call out, who complain, even those who thank the golf gods after a "lucky" shot have no real clue who the gods are or what they're all about.

Did you know that golf gods didn't even exist until 1822? Did you know that some of them work only part-time? That one golf god has a learning disability? Of course you didn't, yet you, along with so many others, talk about them as if they were second cousins.

This book will set you straight. If you want to call on them for help when you need it or if you want to appease one you've accidentally offended, you must learn how to do that.

Like everyone else I talked about the golf gods, telling my friend Jim that they were on his side when he made a long putt but I really didn't mean it. I heard TV announcers talk about them too, but I never figured they really existed.

They do exist. Here's how we got connected.

To avoid cleaning the garage one rainy Saturday I decided to see if I could golf-googlewhack, that is, enter something about golf into the Google search engine and get only one return. The classic way of playing is to enter just one word or name, but to allow myself a chance of winning I limited myself to no more than six words. I tried "golf-bogey-home-runs" and got 305,000 responses. Not very good. So I tried "golf-ballet-tree-sap" and faced 51,400. The idea of googlewhacking using golf seemed impossible. Then I entered "golf-dead-Abraham-Lincoln-concrete," and in 0.37 seconds got a list of 13,400 returns. I was going in the right direction, but not yet close to getting only one response.

I thought for a minute. Google is surreal enough, maybe we could go mystical. I entered "golf-gods-who-what-how-appease." I scored. Only one return. I had golf-googlewhacked. I clicked on the hyperlink.

I was taken to a site that screamed "FREE DOWNLOAD," with a flashing yellow button. That's all there was, just this flashing yellow button that read "FREE DOWNLOAD CLICK HERE." I was feeling adventurous, my virus protection was up-to-date, what the heck. I clicked "DOWNLOAD."

A dialogue box appeared. I had only one option; "open," so I opened. What I got was an Adobe document entitled *The Golf Gods: Who They Are, What They Want, and How to Appease Them*, pretty much exactly what I had googled. So far, so good. I had googlewhacked, and now I was entering the world of the golf gods. Not bad for a dreary Saturday afternoon. After I checked out a few pages it looked like the material might make for interesting reading. I hit Print, and my printer clicked into action. As I listened to the paper shuffle through the printer I wondered, free book download from the Web? Does that sound legit? Somewhere, someone was going to have to pay something to somebody. Two hundred plus printed pages later I'm deep in my armchair reading about all sorts of stuff, from the origin of the game to why Tiger does what he does.

I'd read the whole thing by Sunday night. The last page had a phone number and the request, "Please call." Here goes the scam, I said to myself. I dialed the number and got one of those phone tree things: "If you liked the book, press one. If you didn't like the book, press two."

I pressed one.

"If you consider the golf gods to be an interesting possibility, press one. If you think the golf gods don't exist, press two."

I pressed one again.

"If you would like to test the golf gods, press one." So far no one had asked me for any money.

I pressed one a few more times. Basically the idea was that I could test the golf gods the next time I played by picking one to help me for eighteen holes to see what happened. I clicked "test." I chose the golf god of bunkers because I'm terrible on shots out of the sand, and I seem to be in it five or six times a round. I became a registered golf god tester.

The next round I played I wrote the name of the golf god of bunkers, "Chit," on my scorecard and headed out to the first tee. Seventeen holes later I was playing to my handicap and had not been in the sand all day. Naturally, I put my approach shot on 18 deep into the greenside bunker on the right. Could I expect a miracle? I blasted out to within two feet and sank the putt, miracle enough for me. Was I now a believer? I called the number I was supposed to call after the test.

"If your test was positive, press one." I pressed one. If this was a scam, it was a good one. After a couple more "press ones" I was prompted, "If you want to make some money, press one." Here we go, I thought, time to pay the piper. I was not going to give them any credit card numbers, my address or my social security number, or anything else. But if they wanted me to mail in a few bucks for the book I was certainly willing to do that.

Then I was told to "press one" to switch to an automated voice system. Pretty expensive scam, I thought, but I pressed "one" for the automated system. After a series of questions and my "yes" and "no" answers, I was asked, "Would you like to own this book?"

Why couldn't they have asked me that question twenty minutes ago? I would have bought it.

I answered, "Yes."

"Would you like to publish this book?"

"What?"

"Would you like to publish this book?"

"I don't understand."

"Do you believe in the golf gods?"

"Ah, yeah, sure."

"Would you like others to know about them?"

"Okay."

"The book you read should be available to others."

"It's online. What more do you want?"

"Online doesn't have the dignity this book deserves. It should be a hardback for inclusion in people's libraries."

The penny dropped. "I get it. You want me to pay for publishing the book."

"No. We want you to get the book published by a reputable golf book publisher. You may freely enjoy any royalties that accrue."

This very odd discussion with a voice-activated computer went on for about ten minutes. I heard a lot of stories and got my questions answered. Why me? Why this way? Why now? In the end I agreed to send my printout of the book to a publisher as if it were my own work. But before I sent it I checked with my lawyer friend Sid about copyrights. What he told me was not good. Anything printed is automatically copyrighted. It doesn't have to be registered anywhere. Unless someone signed over the rights to what I had, it wasn't mine.

I called the number again.

"If you are concerned about copyright, press one."

I went through a quick series of pushing ones and learned that the Web site was now closed. I had the only copy of the material, and I should do what I had been asked to do. So I did.

I sent the copy to Ann Arbor Media Group, the people who publish golf classics. Immediately a guy named Skip sent me a contract. They published the book you are now holding exactly as I got it, plus a few of my own additions the golf gods said I could make. I have the official copyright. The Web site no longer exists. The phone number no longer works. It seems like everything is okay.

Before you start reading there are some things I need to tell you, things I learned from my automated telephone conversations, and my thoughts about all this.

I'm a religious guy, I believe in God, and I don't see how these golf gods fit into anything. They explain it, but I'm still not sure. It's like there are two worlds, logic and faith, and somehow this group is in between. There's no worship involved, but they have supernatural powers. They reward good but sometimes reward bad just for the fun of it.

All I really know is that once I learned about who they really are and began doing what they suggest, I've enjoyed playing golf more than ever. I guess that's all that matters.

When you use the information, I suggest you start with some of the lesser gods. You never know what could happen. I still get worried when I'm about to ask Phor for a favor. He's the big cheese and doesn't want anyone to forget it. If you ask him for a favor you better know what you're doing and do it with a truckload of humility. Most of the time that's a good idea. But then sometimes he resents people who come crawling to him. That happens when he thinks it isn't godlike to need people to be nice to him just because he's a golf god.

One thing you have to know from the beginning. When people talk about the golf gods they are exactly right in using the plural. Every golfer at every level is assigned a committee of four golf gods just prior to the first tee shot. Ever wonder about that bad shot on the first tee? In all likelihood the newly formed committee didn't work out their strategy in time to help you. Or maybe they got into an argument and took it out on you. Sometimes, if this committee is a badly coordinated group, you will play in misery all day. And if you get angry at them, they're fully capable of getting angry at you for getting angry at them, and will make things worse.

If you haven't played much golf you might not realize how bad they can make it, even for an innocent player. Bill Hume was with two clients at an upscale daily-fee course. His golf gods committee was in disarray. His first tee shot went out of bounds. His first putt lipped out from two feet. He dunked his approach on two. On three he landed in the fairway bunker, then the green side bunker, and took three to get out of each one. This went on throughout the front nine. At the turn he bought beers and sandwiches for his clients. His smile and composure impressed the heck out of them.

On ten he hit out of bounds again but managed one more smile. One of his clients shook his head and said, "Wow, Bill, the golf gods certainly have it in for you today." Unbeknownst to Bill and his clients, this finally got his golf god committee's attention. For the first time they took interest in the match. This is what Bill said back to his client: "I'm okay. They can do whatever it is they do and I'm not going to be affected." He wanted to keep things light. This was his clients' day and his score, his golf game, really didn't matter. The four golf gods on his committee looked at one another. "I think we've been insulted," one said to the rest. "We didn't mean any harm and he treats us like nobodies," said the second. "What kind of golfer can have his kind of lousy day and still smile?" added the third. "Let's get him," the fourth golf god suggested.

Instantly, the accelerator on Bill's cart stuck as he drove away from leaving his partner at his ball. The cart flew down a steep hill directly toward the ravine on the twelfth hole. He tried to jump out but caught his shirt on the wire basket behind the seat. The cart raced to the edge of the ravine, then over, tumbling through trees and shrubs until finally landing upright in a cloud of dust at the bottom.

In addition to his 67 on the front nine Bill broke his collarbone, broke his left femur, and totaled the cart at a cost of $2,700 (he was found culpable in the subsequent court case). His clients became non-clients after hearing his expletives as he was careening toward the ravine; his clubs were destroyed (and not covered by insurance—refer to the above mentioned court case); and his wife divorced him because he didn't pick her up as promised for their last-chance romantic dinner, and that was the last straw no matter what the reason, she said. As a final insult when he returned home from the hospital, wrapped head to toe in bandages and smelling of antiseptic, his dog bit him on the knee.

Although the golf gods can cause a significant degree of distress, they mostly try to help out. Take, for example, Gene Sarazen. Since you're reading this book you are obviously fond of great golf literature and are probably aware that the Squire invented the sand wedge. Were the golf gods involved in that bit of creative genius? Actually no, Sarazen did that on his own. But they did have an effect later.

One of the golf gods, Maat, who happens to be the great-grandnephew of Bacchus, is the golf god of the nineteenth hole. Maat was in a terrible state during the American Prohibition period as you can well imagine. During this time he felt more and more listless and was seeking a way to have greater impact, more than just tall stories and a few laughs. Things improved after Prohibition was repealed, but it wasn't enough. He consulted with Phor, the chief golf god, who took pity on Maat.

"Why don't you pick out a golfer, decide what you want to do, and I'll help you make something special happen?"

Maat thought this was great. He picked out one of the biggest tournaments of the day, the 1935 Masters Tournament, and chose Gene Sarazen, one of the best golfers. He waited until the final round. Phor and Maat watched from the opening tee shot.

"What do you want to do?" Phor asked as they observed the action.

"Don't know yet," Maat answered. "But I'll think of something in a minute or two."

Sarazen reached the par-five fifteenth hole three strokes back of Craig Wood, the leader.

"I got it," Maat said. "Hole in one on the par five, he wins with a miracle shot."

Phor shook his head. "No can do. Can't have somebody hit it that far, ruin everything. Golf isn't distance, it's accuracy."

Maat watched Sarazen hit his tee ball into the fifteenth fairway. He thought for a moment. "He can reach the green now. We could have him hole from here: A double eagle to tie. How about that?"

Phor thought for a moment. "Like that, but I don't want to do that either. Neither of us is in charge of accuracy. You-know-who has that area, and I sure don't want to step on her toes. Has to be something you can do. I can potentate your power. Think of something you can do and I'll increase your power a hundredfold."

---

## Golf God Factoid

In a poll taken last November—percentages that believed in the golf gods:

- Democrats 81%
- Republicans 79%
- Independents 51%
- Green Party 19%
- Peace/Freedom 92%
- Communist 1 (person)

"I'm in charge of the nineteenth hole. I can make people think they're better than they are."

Phor nodded. "I think I know what we can do."

All the papers the next day described the "Shot heard 'round the world." You know what happened. He sank that 200-plus-yards, 4-wood shot from the fairway for a double eagle, tied the leader, and went on to win the play-off the next day.

But he didn't. In reality, Sarazen parred the hole. He knew his 4-wood would have flown onto the green at too low a trajectory and wouldn't have stayed on the putting surface. Hoping for a birdie on that hole and two more coming in, Sarazen actually laid up with his 5-iron, pitched on, and two-putted for a disappointing par.

Since Phor didn't want to use his direct power to make the great shot happen, he and Maat did the next best thing. Although thousands of people say they saw the shot, in truth there were only a couple of hundred people who were following Sarazen that day. Using his nineteenth hole power of exaggeration, Maat, with Phor's added power, created a mass hypnotic trance in the players, the caddies, the officials, the reporters, and the two hundred–odd spectators. "Four-wood double eagle," he droned over and over, and created the picture in everyone's mind of the ball soaring off the clubface, reaching the green, and bouncing a few times before rolling into the cup. The golf gods can do many things in many ways.

When you think of the golf gods, you might wonder about Tiger Woods. Are the golf gods involved here? Duh. We don't know who may have made a deal with whom, but it sure looks like something supernatural is at work. What is intriguing is what Tiger did a couple of years ago, something that is so rare the golf gods are still talking about it.

Hypothetically, let's say Tiger did make an arrangement with the golf gods, or maybe his father Earl made some kind of an arrangement. If so, you could say that whatever the arrangement was it paid off handsomely. But think about it for a minute. Is it all that great to be all that great? Would you want to be that much better than everyone else? Don't you think it could get lonely at the top?

Pretend you're the best golfer in the world and you're out playing a social game with one of your golf professional buddies. Let's say he's older, had a nice career but no really big wins. Time is running out for your friend. Although he laughs a lot and it seems like he's having fun, you know he's hurting inside. You get the cake and the frosting, he gets a few crumbs. If you really liked the guy what would you do? Would you make a new deal with the golf gods? Say one where you had a couple of "slumps" so your friend could enjoy some of the successes that were promised to you? Would you give up a Masters and maybe even a British Open for a buddy? What a friend you would be if you did! For fun, look up Tiger's record in 1998, and look up Mark O'Meara's record, too, while you're at it. None of this proves anything but it does make you wonder.

Speaking of Tiger, former Tour player and TV announcer Curtis Strange was in on the secret almost from the beginning. "Strange" is a strange name, isn't it? Do you know anyone else with that kind of name? Curtis would probably deny it, but as a kid he wondered how his family got stuck with such a label. He'll tell you something about the family name being translated into English, but if the truth were told, he would admit to "strange" dreams and occasional "strange" thoughts that similarly plagued all the men in the Strange family.

One night early in Tiger's professional career Strange had another of his strange dreams. He dreamt that Tiger's parents realized what a jewel they had in their boy and wanted to do all they could for him. Strange dreamt that while the senior Woods was watching his son on the practice tee one day, he looked to the heavens and said, "Golf gods, here he is." They were listening, and because they also saw a pure heart and Earl's good intentions (especially compared to some of the then current tennis parents) they shone their light on the young phenom.

The day after his strange dream Curtis Strange was in the TV broadcast booth. He watched Tiger hit a Tiger-type shot and let it slip: "There is the next golf god." Asked about the comment later he denied saying it. "Next golf guy," is what he insisted he said. Yeah, right.

# The Beginning

Golf gods didn't exist until 1822. They were around, sort of. They were around like a book on a bookshelf is around, like a memory is around, or like your breakfast burrito is around late in the afternoon. In the modern era the old gods like Zeus and Apollo exist only as amusing artifacts of cultures long gone. Except for the few remaining true believers. Except for deep in as-yet-uncharted reaches of the world. Except for those times late at night when the boundary between real and unreal becomes turned around. Think of the golf gods as hibernating until a call was heard.

This call was faint, but clear.

In 1822 not much was happening in the Western world. Louis Pasteur was born as was Sir Francis Galton, and a few other notables also first saw the light of day. Skin was transplanted for the first time. James Monroe was the U.S. President, and Pius VII was the Pope. Jean Champollion deciphered Egyptian hieroglyphics by translating the Rosetta Stone. Franz Schubert left his Eighth Symphony unfinished. Also in 1822, Brazil successfully declared its independence from Portugal. In Scotland the Caledonian Canal opened. Otherwise in the grand scheme of things the world was quiet.

In the smaller world of golf not much was happening either. By 1822 some clubs were planning centennial celebrations. The feathery ball would still be used for another twenty-five years. And Old Tom Morris was just a toddler.

Most golf was played by two men (sometimes women) in informal matches over the public green. In one such match over the links at Musselborough the golf gods first came into being.

The match was between Harold Higby, a history professor at the local university, and Robert (Bert) Dweem, a dairy farmer. The pair often played against each other, and the stakes were always tuppence. Over their many matches Bert might have been up by a couple of shillings, or maybe not.

The match was dead even on the seventeenth when Bert hit a tee shot that flew high and long, at least 160 yards. Professor Higby was awed. "Ah, Bert, that truly was a shot for the gods."

*Phor*

Miles away, about 1,500 miles, Shega sensed a ripple in the fabric of the spirit world. He was a minor god of a minor Eastern European cult. Over a few hundred years worshippers had declined from a high of 18,000 to less than a couple of backward families. Shega focused his attention on the matches being played over the links. Even from a distance he felt the awe that man can express at the divine, yet there was no god being worshipped, no sacrifice being made.

This was something he had never seen before. A struggle between sportsmen, but there was no umpire. The players competed against one another but called penalties on themselves. Character was being called to the fore, just as in daily life. Play was intense. Money was often involved. Cheating could occur. Pride often outwrestled logic. The cold, the wind, the rain often added significant misery. He was astounded. Here, Shega realized, he could be the supreme being in a microcosm of the universe. He was interested. He applied for the position, scored highest on the test, and became Phor, the first golf god.

His first official act was to thank the professor. The match was still square on the last green. Professor Higby faced a forty-foot triple-breaking putt to win the hole. When it rolled smack into the center of the cup, Bert laughed and said, "Now there was a putt for the gods." Little did he know. Something good for every golfer had just begun.

# Now

Excluding Tiger Woods, who may or may not be a golf god, there are twenty-three golf gods. Tiger is excluded because he cannot be an active golf god while he is playing professionally, or so we're told, anyway. At one time there was a high of thirty-nine active golf gods, but some have retired and have not been replaced. One still holding out is the golf god who was in charge of stymies. One of the grateful retirees was responsible for wooden shafts. There is considerable precedent for a golf god to retire. Dupta, the golf god of water, for example, decided one day to retire, and in a huff it seems he granted all his power to a small fish he named Terrnor.

When golf gods transfer power they lose all of their own completely. The recipient, however, receives the granted powers in degrees either lesser or greater. This "mutant" quality of the transfer keeps things hopping in the golf god world. The golf god fish called Terrnor seems to have less power than did Dupta. This means that there is leftover power hovering around, waiting to attach itself to a lucky golf god. When and how this happens is anyone's guess. One day a golf god can just do more than the day before.

It is not all that common for living mortals to acquire golf godness from a golf god. Besides Terrnor only five or six others have been promoted from the ranks, as it were. One was Tankwa, a native of India in the latter days of the nineteenth century who had raised fifty-nine foster children and who has already retired from being a golf god. Another was Whinsomch, who, interestingly enough, was a spoiled brat in the midst of his terrible twos when elevated to golf god status due to an unfortunate miscalculation.

## *Golf God Factoid*

During the late 1990s golf god Hesta lost 35 pounds on the North Beach diet and has regained only five pounds since.

Mostly, the ranks of golf gods are filled with minor gods from dying religions, along with a few lucky members of the waiting list kept in heaven for those who want to be more active than the norm in the meadows of celestial contentment. If he is in an expansive mood, Phor decides who becomes a golf god and who doesn't. If he's in a bad mood he either closes the door for a half-century or so or has Hesta make the decision. She is the top female golf god in charge of making sure things are done well and beautifully, and, of course, of handling anything Phor neglects to do.

There is no magic in the number twenty-three. Phor was first and was happy handling everything until Hesta asked if she could join him. Hesta was the mortal sister of one of the ancient Greek gods. Because of her bloodline she had a lot of options and took her time choosing. She liked the idea of golf and also thought that Phor might make good husband material. Once she was in the picture, like so many women in the history of civilization, she found many things that needed to be improved and encouraged Phor to keep adding to the golf god population. It seemed a natural thing, she observed, to have a special golf god for all the new women golfers who had no clue about the swing. So for all those women whose swings mimic the action of chopping wood, for all those women who push daintily at the ball through what they have no clue is called the impact zone, and for all those women who spend more time coordinating their outfits than practicing putting, golf god Sarah Winston joined the forces.

Of special note is Chit. His existence arose out of thin air—spontaneous generation. Chit is the golf god of bunker play. As the game grew, especially in the late 1920s, more and more players found themselves in more and more bunkers. More golfers in more bunkers meant more swings, a lot more swings. To the golf gods the air was filled with the same sound, like the harmony of a covey of quail winging it out of the bushes. The golfers all cried the same cry as yet another swing yielded a mouthful of sand and a ball that remained stoically in place. Phor called the existing golf gods together one day and had them concentrate on the word all the players used when they were in the sand. After only a few minutes a new golf god appeared and was of course named Chit.

As with Chit, all the golf gods except Phor and Hesta have specialties. Bok is the golf god of the swing, for example while Bacysos controls holes in one. Any golf god, however, can affect any part of any player's game. The committee assigned to each player has significant impact, at least in theory. The committee has to be well formed and paying attention for maximum effect. Any interested golf god can voice an opinion or throw in an action or two, and your guardian golf god has considerable sway. But it is complicated.

There are golf god vacations to consider, inattention, trying to do too much, part-time golf gods, golf gods with various disabilities, sabotage, playing favorites, new golf gods, veteran golf gods—anything that can affect any human endeavor seems to occur in the world of the golf gods.

Bok exemplifies what can happen. As the golf god of the swing, Bok has to be strong and vigilant, and he usually is. But with so many playing the game these days he can't be everywhere at once. Have you ever had your swing mysteriously disappear? Bok was there for you, then had to go do something else. In fact, here's a tip. If you want to play your absolute best golf, watch a major tournament in the morning like the U.S. Open and play that afternoon. Bok is intensely interested in professional swings in the major tournaments. After focusing all his attention on something like the Open, for the rest of the day he sits back enjoying a martini and infusing the rest of the world with great swing thoughts. This works especially well if you live in a time zone west of the tournament site.

To play your best most of the time you'll have to familiarize yourself with the golf gods and do what you can to determine who might be on your committee for the day's play, who might be available to help you during the round, and which golf god you should call on for specific help during play. You'll also have to guess if any golf god has it in for you and appease him/her/it as best you can.

Statisticians will tell you that with twenty-three golf gods and four to a committee, there are thousands upon thousands of possible combinations. Well, yes and no. Some golf gods refuse to be on committees with certain other golf gods. And often two together will veto certain other golf gods. But count on there

*Hesta*

being many more golf god combinations than golf games you'll play in a lifetime, so the likelihood of getting the same committee twice is remote—which is both good and bad.

You will also have the opportunity to choose a guardian golf god. This is a golf god you studied and decided is the right one for you and your game. You can call on your guardian golf god at any time for anything.

In addition to the committee you're assigned and your guardian golf god, at various times other golf gods will become involved. There are golf gods interested in emotions, thoughts, and situations. That doesn't mean that they will be there when you have a certain emotion or thought, or when you find yourself in a specific situation. They show up when they want to show up. They do what they want to do. Sometimes what they want to do will be aimed squarely at you, sometimes at another golf god, and sometimes what they do is just because, and it's not aimed at anyone.

My advice is to get to know the important golf gods and the ones that might be most interested in your type of game. Learn what they want and how to give it to them. Learn to pick up the signs of who might be on your committee. Basically, pay as much attention to the golf gods as you do picking out your socks in the morning, and I promise you your game will become much more enjoyable.

If you read this book and want to appease the golf gods, you get some beneficence for mere effort. You will get maximum help from them if you call them by name aloud, if you do little favors for them, if you introduce them to your playing companions and treat them in all the thoughtful ways you would treat a valued but invisible friend.

# The Hereafter

The future of golf goddom is good. The game continues to be one of honor. That bodes well. The game borders on the spiritual at times. That also attracts a lot of interest from experienced deities who may want to get into the golf god gig. This is good for golfers. Phor and especially Hesta are interested in adding to the number and power of the golf gods. And, last but certainly not least, a number of current players and others involved in golf are getting long in the tooth, ready to put their names on that waiting list in the sky.

Can you imagine the kind of golf god Arnold Palmer would make? There is talk of putting his name at the top of the list for the next opening once he gets to where he needs to be (but not, we hope, for a long, long time). Phor and Hesta already have an idea. There isn't a golf god for the common player. Wouldn't that be something, standing on the first tee, knowing that the King was watching over you?

Something similar happened recently, but in a soft, almost delicate way. When golf teacher Harvey Penick died, he too went to the top of the list kept in heaven. Being the humble and kindly man he always was, he shook his head and declined the honor. "That isn't for me," he said with a smile. "But there is something I'd like to see happen." In response, Whinsomch, the god of professional golf, forgot about himself for a time and shone on the efforts of one Ben Crenshaw at that year's Masters. That was all the man asked for, a well-regarded title for one of his students. Hesta burst into tears as the last putt dropped. So did the gentle old man watching from above. So did Ben. So did the TV announcers. So did everybody watching. It was the golf gods at their best.

At the other end of the spectrum are the golf demons. It's a given that golf will still be saddled with them in the future and probably in ways that are worse than what we have now. The demons are manifestations of the underbelly of golf and life. They get their power from evil forces, from misguided efforts, from gross negligence, from disregard, from cheaters and sandbaggers. There are three: Kcom, who feeds off your deepest wishes and fears, Orgo, who thrives on neglect, and Minerv, who responds most strongly to dishonor.

In the early days, far earlier than even Phor's beginning, the world had seven demons: pride, envy, gluttony, lust, wrath, greed, and sloth. In its own early days, golf had no demons of its own; the game was too simple, the rules made up by convention or agreement among the players. Small wagers usually didn't arouse any of the deadly sins. When they did, the offender was quickly identified and would never again have the opportunity of a game with the locals.

When clubs were formed, when tournaments were organized, when prizes became gold or silver rather than a few bob, some of the world's ogres found a new home on the links. Dozens, then hundreds, finally thousands of the spirit world's worst sought golfers, club makers, grounds keepers, and anyone else connected to the game to find an edge, any advantage that would spell ruin for one demon and ill gotten glee for the other. There was no honor among this horde. Through deceit, terror, and even cannibalism the many small evils in golf became three immense ones, those we are stuck with today.

Although Kcom, Orgo, and Minerv have different appetites, all three do exactly the same thing. Like leeches, they suck the goodness out of the game and out of golfers.

New players are easy prey. These people come from a culture that does not praise the golf gods but worships modern deities like fast, easy, and fun. They expect golf to change to suit them and not the other way around. Kcom and Orgo are right there to encourage this belief.

---

## Golf God Factoid

There has been a total of 56 golf gods since their inception in 1822. Of those no longer golf gods, all but one retired. Stymie (actual name of the golf god of stymies) is refusing to retire and is on life support.

---

Kcom loves all this controversy over clubs and balls. "Shouldn't such a hard game be made more fun and easier for beginners?" he whispers in everyone's ears. ("He" is used only to make reading easier. The golf demons have no gender, just as they have no souls.) Kcom is interested in getting fat. "Easy" is his favorite word. "Winning" is a close second. A "winning is the only thing" mentality makes him drool. A golfer cheating to win puts him over the top, same as it does Minerv.

There are a number of scary things about the golf demons. One is their influence off the course. Once they are a force within the player, every act of selfishness during the game increases the chance of the same thing happening in daily life.

Another fearsome reality is that any one demon is stronger than any one golf god, including Phor. Collectively, the golf gods could overcome all three demons, but the likelihood of the golf gods getting organized enough to do that is small. Plus, they don't often all come in contact with each other, so any kind of war between them is unlikely.

A third problem is that other demons exist that influence the golf demons, and if all the world's demons could ever cooperate we'd have huge problems. Imagine if the tennis demons and the golf demons worked together. Or what if the demons of politics and demons of golf made a pact? Wouldn't that be awful?

However, the more that golfers contribute to the increase in number and power of the golf gods, and the more we can defend against the influence of the golf demons, the better our game will be. The task is monumental but must be taken on. If we golfers don't do it, no one will.

Next thing to do is determine if you have been affected by the golf gods. It's not necessarily a bad thing if you have; they realize that you probably weren't aware of all the times they provided help and you offered no thanks whatsoever.

# Golf Gods Quiz

How to determine whether the golf gods have been in your life. Keep track of your number of "Yes" answers.

1. Have you ever hit the ball so well that it seemed like you hardly swung?     Yes   No
2. Did you ever have the feeling you were going to make a putt, then did?     Yes   No
3. Have you ever "lost" your swing for no reason?     Yes   No
4. Have you dreamt about playing golf?     Yes   No
5. Do you have a "lucky" ball marker?     Yes   No
6. Do you have a favorite brand of golf ball?     Yes   No
7. Do you suddenly get thirsty just after finishing the eighteenth hole?     Yes   No
8. Do you seem to hit one club better than the others?     Yes   No
9. Are you sometimes afraid to hit a shot?     Yes   No
10. Do you sometimes lose confidence on the course?     Yes   No
11. Have you read *Golf in the Kingdom* or *The Way of Golf?*     Yes   No
12. Have you ever successfully predicted a golf shot?     Yes   No
13. Have you ever "lost" a ball in the middle of the fairway?     Yes   No
14. Did you ever make a hole in one?     Yes   No
15. Did you ever make a bet you couldn't afford and won?     Yes   No
16. Did you meet your spouse on the golf course?     Yes   No
17. Have you ever holed a shot out of a bunker?     Yes   No

18. Have you had an amorous adventure on
    the golf course?                                          Yes    No
19. Have you successfully used a golf tip
    found in a golf magazine?                                 Yes    No
20. Do you have a favorite course?                            Yes    No
21. Have you ever played an entire round
    with the same golf ball?                                  Yes    No
22. Have you ever mentioned the golf gods
    out loud to someone?                                      Yes    No
23. Did that someone in the question above
    comment positively?                                       Yes    No
24. Have you played in the rain and not been
    hit by lightning?                                         Yes    No
25. Have you ever hit the ball well off the
    first tee with others watching?                           Yes    No
26. Did you ever think you would bogey a
    hole but instead got par?                                 Yes    No
27. Have you ever just turned on TV and
    immediately seen a great shot?                            Yes    No
28. Did you pay money for this book?                          Yes    No
29. Was this book a gift?                                     Yes    No
30. Have you ever experienced great
    contentment after a round of golf?                        Yes    No

If you answered "Yes" to at least four of these questions, it's possible you've had contact with one of the golf gods. If you answered "Yes" to more than seven, then it's almost a certainty that you and the golf gods have connected somewhere along the way. If this is the case, then you need to pay very close attention to what's inside this book. To help your budding relationship with the golf gods, the next section answers some questions you may have.

# Frequently Asked Questions

*I play golf only one or two times a year. Do I have golf gods assigned to me?*

Yes. Even if you play only once in your life, you will be assigned a committee like everyone else and may have your game influenced by other golf gods.

*Why do I often play very well after not playing for a long time?*

This occurs because golf gods want you to play more frequently. Committee gods assigned to you are aware of what you've done in the past. They are also aware of your motivation to play when you return to golf. You may notice that your expectations are lower if you haven't played in a while. The golf gods like to reward that kind of humbleness.

*Do some people frequently have the same golf god oversee their play?*

Yes. Sometimes golf gods have affection for certain players. Although they may not be on that day's committee they watch over the player and often get involved in different ways. Of course, the opposite can also happen. A golf god can get irritated at a player and make that person suffer game after game after game. Your guardian golf god is also there for you (most of the time).

*Do the golf gods like kids?*

Love 'em. The only way kids can get into trouble with the golf gods is to swear a lot or to be mean to other kids. Kids can get as mad as wet hens or even cheat a little to protect their developing egos, but boy, watch out for meanness. Golf instructors might want to know that the golf gods consider only three things relevant to teaching kids the swing: the grip, balance, and fun.

## *Golf God Factoid*

Like many of the minor spirits, golf gods expire when no one needs them, asks for them, or thinks about them for a 188-day period. They simply dematerialize on the 189th day—painlessly and without awareness. They can safely retire any time during or before this period and live happily for eternity.

*Do the golf gods play golf?*

Some do, some don't. Of those that play golf some play regular golf just like we mortals do, while others just play one shot. Chit, the golf of bunker play, for example, hits only bunker

*Chit*

shots. He has a current streak of 114 million sand shots in a row going into the hole.

*What happens to golf gods when they're no longer golf gods?*
There is a special place called Gowondaland where they may retire. No one but the golf gods knows what this place is like, but it's safe to assume it's pretty nice.

*If I want to play a certain shot, like hit a knock-down out of the trees, do I ask for help from a specific golf god?*
That depends. If your committee is fully functional, that isn't necessary. All you do is ask for their help out loud, and if they're willing you're in good shape. If, however, you think you're stuck with a dysfunctional committee, you may be wise to pick out a golf god who is interested in the type of shot you want to play and ask for help. It's almost always a good idea to ask for help from a golf god who has provided help in the past, no matter what their special interest. They can help everywhere. Unless you happen to go to the same well too often—then this idea doesn't work. If you seek help from a golf god not on that day's committee you also risk offending the committee, so you'd be advised to thank your committee out loud before seeking help from someone who is not on it. The trouble is it's hard to know exactly who is on your committee that day.

*Do the golf gods know the answer to life's important question?*
Yes, they do. And they are more than willing to help you discover it.

*Can one golf god cancel out the effects of another golf god?*
Oh, yes. This happens all the time. Committee members on an unorganized committee are canceling out each other's intentions on almost every shot. Sometimes this is deliberate, as when the committee members are fighting each other, but this can happen simply because they have different intentions. The opposite can happen, too. Two or more golf gods can want the same thing and double or even triple the outcome. Holes in one on par 4s are common examples.

*If I start play with one committee, does this committee stay with me for all eighteen holes? What if I play thirty-six or more?*

Each set of eighteen holes is considered one round, and you have the same committee for one round. Any part of a round is considered one round. But eighteen holes is the committee's limit. This means that if you play twenty holes you have one committee for the first eighteen and a second committee for the next two holes.

*What happens if I'm in a play-off? Shouldn't this count as the same round?*

The same thing occurs every time you play more than eighteen holes. After eighteen holes, play-off or not, you get a new committee. The USGA is well aware of this procedure on the part of the golf gods, and in their wisdom chose an eighteen-hole play-off for the U.S. Open Championship. The USGA does not want the winner decided by an unorganized committee and knows that an eighteen-hole play-off gives each competitor a better chance at having a working committee behind his/her play. Why they don't tell the world of their reasoning about an eighteen-hole play-off when people complain about it is anyone's guess.

*Do different golf gods have different levels of power?*

Absolutely. Major golf gods have greater power than major-minor golf gods. The major-minor golf gods have more power than minor golf gods. You might also want to know that the power they use is relative. Less experienced golf gods sometimes use more power than they need, sometimes less. If the golf god is a specialist, say, a specialist of putting like the golf god Oopmon, and a lot of people are putting at the same time, his power is somewhat reduced for each individual. If fewer players are putting, he has more effect. The gods also can have a stronger effect if the player is willing to allow it. This happens if the golfer can clear the mind of thoughts, thus allowing the golf god easier access and ultimately more control over the results. Clearing the mind is one of the reasons why sports psychologists dwell on a preshot routine to help the player relax, which is exactly the right thing to do. Few of these masters of the mental game,

*Oopmon*

however, give the golf gods any of the credit for the benefits of this approach.

*Do golf gods have power off the course?*

They can if they like. Golf gods usually focus only on what is happening on the course. However, they are known to influence what you think and feel about golf and your game when you're not playing. They also can insert themselves into your being in various ways and control your thoughts and feelings. You won't know when this happens, but often people will remark afterwards that you were acting strangely. Golf god Obsissa seems to like to do this a lot.

*What is the difference between golf gods and golf demons?*

For the most part, golf gods want you to enjoy golf. They cause trouble when they fight among themselves, when they get angry at you, and sometimes just for a little fun. The golf demons want to make your life miserable. They don't like golf or golfers. Any harm they can do is a plus for them. It's important to understand that your actions while playing golf and in your daily life can increase the power of the golf demons. The golf gods try to make golf a sanctuary, while the demons make everything a battleground.

*Can golf gods fall in love?*

Oh, yes, they do it all the time. They can fall in love with each other, with mortals, even with golf courses, golf shots, and golf clubs. As a group they're pretty indiscriminate. You'd get that way too. As a golf god you don't have to worry about getting punished for anything—the sky's the limit. Marriage is rarely in the offing, however, so if you are approached by a golf god for a good time it might be wise to treat the overture as you would a rabid dog—walk slowly backward until you can get out of there.

*Can anyone become a golf god?*

Theoretically yes, but the chances are slim. If you're not already a god of some sort you have two avenues. You could marry a golf god and hope your golf god spouse gives you power, or you could ask to be put on the waiting list after you die. By sheer chance a golf god might give you powers like what happened to Terrnor, the fish, but this is extremely rare. Even if you're already a god you'd have to hope either that an opening occurs or that a new position is created.

*I don't believe in golf gods. Can you prove that they exist?*

It's one of those things you have to experience. You may want to observe fellow players. Do they talk to the ball while it's in flight? Do they plead and beg sometimes while the ball is moving? Do unexplainable things sometimes happen? If you observe well, you will understand. But you don't have to. It's your game. Yet you might want to take advice from French mathematician and theologian Blaise Pascal (d. 1662) who put forward this "wager":

> If there is a God, He is infinitely incomprehensible, since, having, neither parts nor limits, He has no affinity to us. We are then incapable of knowing either what He is or if He is . . . you must wager. It is not optional. You are embarked. Which will you choose then? Let us weigh the gain and the loss in wagering that God is. Let us estimate these two chances. If

you gain, you gain all; if you lose, you lose nothing. Wager then without hesitation that he is.

Basically, if you believe in the golf gods and they exist, you've gained more enjoyment from golf. If you believe in the golf gods and they don't exist, you've lost nothing. By the way, the golf gods don't appreciate people talking to their golf balls and expecting something good to happen. They prefer being communicated with directly, not through an inanimate object. Remember that.

*Do golf professionals respect the golf gods?*
You better believe it. Golf professionals are independent, self-serving, and self-reliant, but when it comes to doing everything they can to score well they do everything they can, including pleasing the golf gods. Do you see them giving golf balls to kids sitting nearby? The only reason to do that is to appease the golf gods. Pros know that works every time. Next time you see a pro perform a charitable act, go up and ask him or her which golf god is being appeased. You might learn something.

*Do the golf demons do anything good for the game?*
Ultimately they do, but it takes a long time. It's like survival of the fittest, and like what happens when a parasitic plant attaches itself to a tree in the forest. Eventually the forest overcomes this scourge and is stronger for it. When a demon infests a player, the player becomes more and more a curse to golf and eventually to daily living. Hitler is a good example. He played golf for a short time as a teenager. Within half a dozen rounds he was so demonized that he quit golf and became a Chancellor. This led to significant individual tragedies and worldwide horror. But eventually the world recovered and became a better place. Less drastic but still unsettling effects can be seen in many of today's politicians who play golf. You can easily tell which ones have the most demons inside them.

*Will it help my game to think about the golf gods when I'm not playing golf?*
This is a difficult question to answer. It depends on what you mean by "think about." The golf gods are sensitive to balance.

They certainly want you to think about them and golf, but not to the degree that it affects other important areas of your life. Spend at least some time thinking about your family, your job, and your friends. A 65:35 ratio of golf gods to everything else might be a good place to start and see what happens from there.

*My friends don't believe in golf gods. Should I do something?*

If you like your friends and want the best for them, why wouldn't you want to help them benefit from the golf gods? This is what you should do. Let them know you're praying to the golf gods for them. Then make sure that after every good shot they hit you say, "Well, there you go, more help from the golf gods. Didn't I tell you?" If you keep this up long enough and often enough, sooner or later they'll get the point and be very grateful.

---

## Golf God Factoid

A golf hole, the hole in the ground that is the ultimate goal, is exactly 4¼ inches in diameter. Until this standard was established, golf holes were just that, holes in the ground. Phor made sure the legal standard became 4¼ inches because that was the diameter of the goblet he was drinking from when he became a golf god. It's too bad he wasn't drinking out of a bucket or maybe taking a bath.

---

*Sometimes after a bad shot, I use words I probably shouldn't. Am I offending the golf gods?*

Not at all. In fact, they sometimes cause problems just to hear what people might say. However, if you're using those bad words to criticize the golf gods they might fail to see the humor in the situation and get mad, then get even. Be careful.

*Are holes in one controlled by golf gods?*

Totally. The great majority of them are provided exclusively by Bacysos, who has a soft spot for players who carry ball retrievers.

*How can I cure my slice?*

A slice is caused by mistrust. Slicers begin the downswing too early, throwing the hands out away from the body at the beginning of the swing because they feel alone and unloved on the golf course and think they must do everything on their own. Once you believe in the golf gods, truly believe in the golf gods, you will trust them and allow your swing to unfold naturally. You won't be tense. You'll relax and allow your swing to just happen. The golf gods will sing in your ear and guide your hands. Your slice will disappear forever, but only if you truly believe.

*What kind of power do the golf gods really have?*

This is the kind of question that can get a golfer into trouble. The golf gods would want to know, "Why do you ask?" But here is a general answer. Phor and Hesta, the highest golf gods, can turn any golfer into a world champion. They can enable anyone to find great joy on even the worst of days. They can, and often have (especially Hesta), brought two strangers together on the first tee and created two soulmates by the eighteenth. They can also break your heart as easily as snapping a twig. They can take away your golf swing and never return it. Lee Trevino once criticized the golf gods and was hit by lightning. Ian Baker-Finch did the same and hit out of bounds on the first hole of St. Andrews Old Course, the widest fairway in golf (and lost his swing, too). David Duval shot a 59 on the PGA Tour, assumed he did it without golf god help, and was banished for a few years. He should be allowed back at any time.

The major golf gods such as Sarah Winston have slightly less power and mostly in lesser duration. They cannot break your heart so it can never mend, but are able to twist it enough to ruin a round or a week's golfing vacation. On the plus side, these gods have been known to give out holes in one, inspire scores ten strokes less than a person's handicap, and ensure the victory of the occasional PGA championship.

The major-minor golf gods have less power but seemingly a greater degree of creativity. They enable golfers to find their swing just in time to win a match. They are the ones who are often responsible when you leave your golf shoes at home or when you are disqualified because of writing down a four when you honestly meant to write five.

The minor golf gods primarily affect what happens to the golf ball. They can have spurts of power as high as major-minor golf gods, but this is rare. Bounces off a rock in the ocean and back to the fairway (talk with Hale Irwin) can be their doing.

The best way to understand the golf gods' power is to think of the worst thing that ever happened to you on the golf course, multiply that by a hundred, and you'll be in the ballpark. At the same time, think of the best thing that can happen on the course and multiply that by a thousand. They can be nasty sometimes, but they are intent on helping us enjoy the best game we could ever hope to play. They also enjoy the heck out of being golf gods. Who wouldn't?

# The List of Golf Gods

| Name | Sex | Area |
|------|-----|------|
| Phor | M | All of golf |
| Hesta | F | Everything Phor doesn't do |
| Sarah Winston | F | Focus is on women golfers and grace |
| Otom | N/A | Pride |
| Bok | M | Swing |
| Pokkie | M | Pace of play |
| Wooda | 3rd | First tee |
| Oupman | M | Putting |
| Chit | M | Bunkers |
| Maat | M | Nineteenth hole |
| Terrnor | F | Water |
| Faunis | F | Ball on a tee |
| Whinsomch | M | Professional golf |
| Bingo | F | Grip |
| Bango | M | Release |
| Bongo | F | Balance |
| Obsissa | M | Distance |
| Susan | F | Accuracy |
| Bacysos | M | Holes in one |
| Fabu | F | Breaking 100 |
| Nogoeh | M | Protecting par |
| Umuligt | M | Shooting 54 |
| Masfel | N/A | Self-awareness |

# Golf Mysteries Demystified

There are many mysteries in golf. Where did the cry "fore" come from? Why couldn't Sam Snead ever win the U.S. Open? Why does playing through a slow group always result in a humiliatingly bad shot?

These unknowns exist only if you don't understand how the golf gods work. Sometimes they make things happen; other times they allow things to happen.

Take for example the mystery of why a round of golf is eighteen holes rather than, say, twenty, five, or nineteen. Where did eighteen holes come from? There is a charming story that golf has eighteen holes because a bottle of whisky has eighteen shots, and if you take one drink per hole after eighteen holes you've run out of whisky, and if there's no whisky there's no golf.

Well, this idea can't be true if you know anything about the Scots. If one brought a full bottle to the game he would either freely share with his opponent or be shamed into doing it; either way, the bottle would be drained way before the eighteenth hole. And, if the other Scot had any idea a bottle was being brought, he would certainly be thrifty and not bring a second bottle that actually could get them through to the eighteenth hole.

A few people, however, believe that the golf gods made eighteen holes the standard because of their affection for numbers divisible by nine. However, this cannot be the case either, because St. Andrews changed its number of holes in the mid-eighteenth century, while the golf gods didn't come into being until the early nineteenth century.

A more credible story is that St. Andrews reduced their number of holes from the original twenty-two to eighteen because golfers thought the first and last few holes were too short and should be made into two holes. St. Andrews, having the most glory and influence at the time, was emulated by other courses and the standard became eighteen holes.

Since 1822 the golf gods have gotten involved in their share of mysteries but have not been involved in others. This section explores some of golf's mysteries and demystifies them. They are in random order so as not to offend any of the golf gods.

# Why Hall of Fame Golfer Sam Snead
# Never Won the U.S. Open Championship

The fact is that Sam Snead was one of the greatest players on the American PGA Tour. He won more events than anyone else, an estimated 135 worldwide, with 84 of them on the American tour. He had a swing as smooth as syrup. His longevity is legendary. He began winning on tour in 1938 at the Oakland Open and didn't stop until 1967, when he was almost fifty-three. He won three Masters, three PGAs, and the 1946 British Open. In the 1979 Quad Cities Open he became the first player to shoot his age (sixty-seven) in a regular tour event. But he never won the U.S. Open.

To understand why, you need only combine two ingredients. One is that Snead was a good old boy, quicker with an off-color comment than diarrhea on a bus. One that can be repeated in a high-class literary golf book such as this one is his comment to a reporter after playing in the Open in 1953, where he finished six strokes behind Ben Hogan. When asked if he was tight, Snead replied, "Tight? I was so tight you couldn't a drove flax seed up my ass with a knot maul." His stories at the Champions Dinners before the Masters reddened the cheeks and burned the ears of many in attendance. Many of his comments involved the fairer sex.

The other ingredient in this recipe of self-destruction is the sensibilities of golf god Sarah Winston. Poor Sam had the misfortune of beginning his career and establishing his reputation when Ms. Winston was fighting hardest for the rights of new women golfers. She was mortified by his attitude. No way, she thought, should Sam Snead reach the highest level of golf. No way, she decided, would she allow him to represent himself as the Champion Golfer in the United States.

Ms. Winston went to her "parents" Phor and Hesta and pleaded her case. Hesta was immediately supportive. Phor was not. He, if truth be told, enjoyed Snead's sense of humor. Phor even made sure that Snead won his first Masters so the Champions dinner would be a much livelier affair. After Snead won,

*Sarah Winston*

Phor never missed the dinners that Snead attended. Unfortunately, Hesta knew of Phor's affection for Snead and said, "You already made sure he won the Masters, and you certainly can help him win other major tournaments. I declare that we should compromise and allow whatever championships you desire for him but one, the U.S. Open." Ms. Winston said she agreed with that. Then they both stared at Phor until he gave in.

Poor Sam began suffering the suffering of the damned (which, of course, he was). In the 1937 U.S. Open at Oakland Hills, Sam shot only one stroke over the prior scoring record and was relaxing in the clubhouse while the others struggled their way in. But he was caught by Ralph Guldahl, who broke the record and beat young Sam. Two years later he had two holes to go and a highly probable two-stroke victory. Two pars would do it. On No. 17 he three-putted sloppily (thanks to Ms. Winston). Sam needed par to beat Byron Nelson, who had already finished, but Craig Wood and Denny Shute were still playing behind him. Sam thought a birdie was essential. He gritted his teeth. Ms. Winston smiled.

He pulled his tee shot into the rough. From the deep grass he attempted too much by trying to power a brassie. He topped the ball, which rolled into a bunker. Here, Snead caused another problem. He called on the golf god of bunkers in an angry way. Chit made him pay with two shots to get out, and made him pay some more by having that ball land in a greenside bunker. Snead played this shot forty feet from the hole, then three-putted. Sam was cooked in his own juices.

Snead lost another chance when he and Lew Worsham were in a play-off for the 1947 Open. On the last hole of the play-off, with the score tied, both were about two and a half feet from the hole. Snead was about to putt first when Worsham stopped him. "Are you sure you're away?" This led to a protracted discussion and finally a measurement by an official. Snead was indeed away. He putted first and missed. Worsham didn't. End of story.

It's too bad that Snead was active when he was. By the 1960s Sarah Winston was much more hip to a lot of things, including going with the flow and letting people be what they're gonna be. But she wasn't when Sam Snead was at his best. Poor damned Sam.

## Why Journeyman Orville Moody Did Win the U.S. Open Championship

Orville Moody won the U.S. Open in 1969 because Byron Nelson retired too early to win it himself.

In 1945 Byron Nelson set a record that will be very hard to beat. He won eleven consecutive PGA tournaments, eighteen overall. He was thirty-three at the time and at the peak of his career. His record includes the 1937 Masters, the 1939 U.S. Open, the 1940 PGA Championship, the 1942 Masters, and the 1945 PGA Championship. He won a total of twenty-six tournaments during his top years of 1944 and 1945. His average score in 1944 was 69.67. In 1945 he lowered it to 68.33. He was poised for the greatest golf year ever. The golf gods loved him.

He won five events in 1946 and finished second in the U.S. Open. Not quite up to his accomplishments of the year before. This was because many players were returning from World War II, and the golf gods were committed to welcoming them back with good fortune on the links. The plan was to make it up to "Lord Nelson" by giving him his greatest year in 1947, with many more great years to follow. The golf gods had it all mapped out. There was a list of twenty-four majors, all belonging to him. But he retired. The major tournaments he would have won had to go to others. By 1969 the only tournament left in the golf gods' inventory specifically reserved for Nelson was a U.S. Open.

For the golf gods the U.S. Open was indeed "open." None of the golf gods had a clear favorite, none had any agreements to meet, and none had it in for another golf god. All in all that year there was so much going on worldwide that they were paying more attention to the war in Vietnam than to national golf championships. During their usual pre-tournament conference Bok mentioned to Phor that they had one Nelson U.S. Open left over.

"So do we want to use Nelson's last Open this year?" he asked all that were assembled.

"May as well," Bok answered. "We've been giving away at least one of his majors almost every year since '47, may as well get rid of the last one."

## *Golf God Factoid*

Young Tom Morris was once asked to be a golf god on account of his great golf success, especially in the early British Open, and his untimely death. However, his Scottish brogue was so thick Phor couldn't figure out if he accepted or not and hasn't gotten back to him to find out.

"Any takers?"

Setth (who later retired as a golf god in 1973) raised his hand. "There's a war going on, you know."

"I know. I know," Phor said.

"Why don't we give it to an army guy?" Hesta suggested.

The group murmured approval.

"Has to be someone with a connection to Byron, that's the deal, remember," came a voice from the crowd.

"What army player has a connection to Nelson?" Phor asked.

All the golf gods thought back.

"Got it," Bok answered. He has an encyclopedic recall of tournament golf as befits the golf god of the golf swing, especially really good ones. "How's this for a connection? Nelson won his first professional tournament at the Monmouth Country Club in 1935. The army bought the club in 1942. A couple of years ago Lt. Frank Thomas won the All-Army Tournament, beating a sergeant named Orville Moody. Moody is currently playing the tour. Why don't we have Moody win the Open?"

"I like it," Phor replied. "Nelson's first tournament. Army guy's loss at the same place. Nice enough connection. We can make it up to him. Has Moody won anything?"

"Nope."

"Okay. Let's give it to him. One hit wonder?"

Since this was Bok's idea, he had the last say. "Let's not decide now. Give him the Open, then we'll take another look later."

But it seems like they never did get back to ol' Sarge. He never won again on the regular tour. Moody's next best finish in a major tournament was an eighth place in the PGA the same year as his Open triumph at the Champions Golf Club in Houston.

*Bok*

# The True Origin of Golf

As you now know, the golf gods didn't exist as golf gods until 1822. But Phor, due to his interest in being a responsible golf god, decided to go back in history to learn the true origin of the game. Most golfers and even nongolfers understand that golf began in Scotland. Holland claims "Kolf," a game of sticks and a ball aimed at a post, and other countries including China seek to be the place where golf was first played. Phor sought the truth so he could honor the game that had become his. He had to go back a while, almost farther than his powers would allow, for each century of time travel temporarily exhausts about five percent of a golf god's power. It turns out that golf is one of the minor, albeit interesting ironies of history.

The period Phor found himself in is best described by Edward Gibbons in his seminal and almost lyrical *The History of the Decline and Fall of the Roman Empire.*

> In the second century of the Christian era, the Empire of Rome comprehended the fairest part of the earth, and the most civilised portion of mankind. The frontiers of that extensive monarchy were guarded by ancient renown and disciplined valour. The gentle but powerful influence of laws and manners had gradually cemented the union of the provinces. Their peaceful inhabitants enjoyed and abused the advantages of wealth and luxury. The image of a free constitution was preserved with decent reverence: the Roman senate appeared to possess the sovereign authority, and devolved on the emperors all the executive powers of government. During a happy period (A.D. 98–180) of more than fourscore years, the public administration was conducted by the virtue and abilities of Nerva, Trajan, Hadrian, and the two Antonines.

Maybe it was a happy period for some people. It was not a happy period for the officers and men of the Roman legions occupying the far northern reaches of the empire, namely the area known as Caledonii. Early in the Roman conquest of the Britons fierce tribes such as the Votadini, the Novantae, and the Selgovae would attack and retreat. After they were subdued other tribes attacked, eventually requiring the Romans to erect the Antonine Wall between what is now Edinburgh and Glasgow. North of this wall, in the midst of the unrest, was the frontier post of Bearsden. This remote outpost of Roman civility quickly became a constant battlefield. Soldiers would advance across the countryside, pillaging and destroying in attempts to subdue the rabble. Those that remained at the outpost, wives and other camp followers, would sometimes have to repel raids on their own. Life was hard. The niceties of Rome were long forgotten. The women, now unwashed, hair matted, stinking of sweat and filth, their teeth rotting into black stumps, were angry most of the time and berated the men when they returned home without great prizes of gold and silver. The men became barbaric. One of the joys of the campaign was to plunder native camps, find the women, and bring the best-looking ones back to Bearsden.

After a time the Roman wives found themselves being replaced in the affections of the soldiers by the native women. It became a practice for the army to campaign for weeks at a time, return for only a few days, shower attention on the barbarian women, then go off to campaign again. Naturally the Roman wives began to resent this arrangement.

During one extended campaign the women got together to discuss what they could do to get their men back. First, they decided, they had to get rid of the Scots women. This was done easily enough by telling them to leave or they would be hit with sticks, strangled, and then dumped into the nearest loch. But then they had to figure a way to keep the men around. One of them remembered the theme of the classic Greek play *Lysistrata*. In the play by Aristophanes, Greek women were fed up with their warmongering husbands and decided to refuse them sex in an effort to stop the endless battles.

"That's stupid," one replied. "That's the opposite of what we're trying to do."

"Exactly," said another. "We want the men to stay home and pay attention to us."

A third woman lamented, "He unsheathes his sword for everyone but me."

"We have to think of a way to keep them home, rather than roaming around and bringing back all sorts of things."

"We could lose some weight."

They all groaned.

"How about a series of parties?"

"That would be a lot of work, and how could we keep them interested? It has to be something that would keep them occupied for an extended period."

They all pondered for a long time.

"Why don't we invent a game? They seem to like tramping all over the countryside. Why don't we invent a game that has them do that, but return home every night?"

"That's a great idea. But what kind of game?"

"It has to be about length. They're always worried about the length of things."

The others giggled.

"And the game should include putting something in something. They always want to do that too."

More giggling.

"Okay. The game should be tramping over the countryside putting something into something some distance away. Does that sound right?"

They all nodded in agreement.

"And it should enable them to come home every night, and maybe tire them out just a bit so they want to come home."

"Yes, yes. We have to remember that."

"And have nothing to do with war or weapons. There should be nothing to remind them of anything else."

At that moment one of the women dropped a piece of meat. She absentmindedly kicked it toward a nearby dog.

"That's it," her friend cried out. "We'll invent a game of kicking a ball across the countryside.

"Into what?" one asked.

"I don't know," she answered. "A rabbit hole."

"Have to be a small ball."

So they invented a kicking game they called "gaul" in honor of the classy wine-producing province most of them wished to return to. They introduced it immediately to the men when they returned home, as a distraction from the missing Scots women. The men enjoyed the game right away. It was fun kicking the ball away from the others, and the pushing and shoving when they suddenly spotted a rabbit hole was just like the fightin' and fussin' they liked best.

The women noticed that the game they invented was too warlike, reminding the men what they had been sent to this outpost to go out and do. They gathered again.

"We have to change the game."

"Yes. We have to get rid of the team element and the pushing and shoving around the ball."

"I've got it."

"What?" the women asked.

"Instead of teams it's one person against another, and more importantly each has his own ball. No fighting."

"Brilliant."

So the women changed the rules. The men played the new game and enjoyed it very much.

During one game a player found his ball stuck between two rocks. He couldn't kick it. He found a stick and batted it out. "Hmmm," he thought. He took another swipe at the ball and sent it flying twice as far as he could kick it. And thus the game of "gaul" became a game of hitting a small ball into a small hole with an implement ill suited to the task.

However, by the year 180, the Roman government decided to retreat from the far outposts and use Hadrian's Wall as the northern boundary. As the Romans were moving south the Picts moved south as well to fill the gap. The Picts, so named because they "picked" up things as they advanced, picked the new game "gaul" for themselves. Later in the constant love-hate relationship with the Scots who were invading from Ireland, the Picts shared the new game of "gaul" that the Scots, with their guttural growl, mispronounced into "golf."

And there you have it, the true origin of golf straight from Phor's mouth. There is no other way that the game was invented. You can bet your life on it.

# Why Weekend Golfers Are Always Short of the Flag

Put your thinking cap on; this could get confusing.

The IQ of the average golfer has been measured as 112. The IQ of the average human being is 100. The person with an average IQ knows that the American flag is red, white, and blue and is confident that if you buy two forty-cent stamps and give the clerk a dollar, you'll get twenty cents change. The person with an average IQ is not quite sure why you shouldn't give money to a beggar but can usually figure it out. If you asked the person with an average IQ a golf question like:

> *If a golfer can hit a 7-iron 150 yards and a 6-iron 160 yards when there is no wind, what club should the golfer use to hit the ball 150 yards into a twenty-mile-an-hour wind?*

The average person would probably say a 6-iron. However, the average golfer would say 7-iron, just hit it harder.

With an IQ of 112, the golfer is smarter than about three quarters of the population. You would think that with this level of intellectual power the average golfer would soon learn to hit the ball far enough to reach the green and often far enough to be hole high. This isn't the case. Ninety-four percent of weekend golfers' shots to the green are short of the hole. A whopping 60 percent don't even reach the green. You might think this is an ego problem. Consider the very occasional boast "Yep, got there with a 7-iron," seemingly more rewarding than actually getting there with the appropriate club, often a 5-wood. If ego were the problem this chronic underclubbing would be caused most often by the inflated male ego. But research shows that an equal percentage of women players also underclub (and this in spite of their average IQ being 113). So it isn't ego.

Some golf instructors believe that golfers recall their best shots with various clubs and use that distance to choose a club. For example, if average golfer George once hit his 5-iron 170 yards, from then on until he's a hundred years old he swings that 5-iron from 170 yards out unless the green is fifty feet uphill or the wind is fifty miles an hour into his face. Somewhere in his brain he may realize this folly, because he'll tend to swing from his heels to get the distance and never get it ever again. But still he'll try.

If you sat down with someone like George and asked him about the odds of winning the state lottery he'd probably tell you how bad the odds are and that he really didn't expect to win when he bought tickets. During the same conversation you could ask him about reaching the green with his 5-iron from 170 yards away. He'd say, "Sure. That's how far I hit my five. I didn't hit it that well today, though." How can he say he didn't hit it well when he hit the ball 170 yards with this 5-iron only once in his life, and that was five years ago? He knows how probability works. He proved that by knowing the odds of winning the lottery. Do you think he would bet his life on hitting his 5-iron 170 yards? Weirdly enough, he might. Taking too little club all the time must be some sort of mass delusion. Or result from some kind of involvement of the golf gods.

Do you know the story of Sisyphus? What happened in golf is similar. In the ancient days of Greece Sisyphus got himself married a few times, once to a niece and another time to a woman who murdered their two sons because they were foretold to be big trouble. One of his marriages produced Odysseus of *Iliad* fame, but that's another story. What is important about Sisyphus is that he told a minor god, Asopus, where his daughter, abducted and raped by the great god Zeus, could be found. Zeus didn't like being finked on, so he punished Sisyphus by making him roll a huge rock up a hill, and just before he would get it to the top Zeus would make it roll back to the bottom. Sisyphus has been coming up short for more than two thousand years.

In the early days of golf, golfers would hit up to the hole on average 33⅓ percent of the time. They would be long 33⅓ percent of the time and be short 33⅓ percent, just as the laws of probability would dictate. All was well in the world of golf—until Malcolm Maynard arrived on the scene.

Malcolm Maynard was a dirty slimeball of a man. He was five foot two with greasy black hair, grime under his fingernails, and evil in his heart. No one liked him. No one cared if he lived or died, or if they did they hoped he would die. However, as is often the case, he knew something. What he knew in 1903 was that Phor, like the big guy Zeus, made a mistake one day by dallying with a mortal. The mortal was Malcolm's sister Silvia. Silvia was the opposite of her brother. She was as sweet as cornbread and blond, with pouty lips that begged to be kissed. She was also chaste, a churchgoer from the age of five until that fateful afternoon when Phor spotted her having tea at the local hotel in Somerset.

Phor, of course, is a man's god, full of vigor and with a keen eye for the ladies. Rarely would he stray from his true love Hesta, but then there was that day in Somerset.

Silvia sat primly at the table. Her ivory-white lace dress fell gracefully over her knees and down to her ankles, covering all but the tips of her dainty lace-up black shoes. Gazing upon her Phor could scarcely catch his breath. Without hesitation and certainly without thinking of the consequences, he assumed human form, introduced himself, and swiftly won her heart. Before her tea had had a chance to cool, they were in a room, hot with passion and doing things only a god would know how to do. Later she sobbed in his arms, grief-stricken at what she had done and what she had lost. Phor, too, was mortified at what had transpired. He would do anything to make right this tempestuous trespass. Trying to appease her Phor did what any male would do. He tried to talk her out of her feelings.

## *Golf God Factoid*

Golf gods who play golf have an average handicap of plus 58.

"I am Phor, god of golf," he told her, thinking that would mean something.

"I don't care if you're the blooming King of England. You had your way with me and now I'm forever ruined."

"You don't have to tell anyone. No one will know if you don't tell them."

"I know," she cried. "It is enough that I know."

Phor shrugged his shoulders. "What do you want me to do?"

"You're a god. Make me as I was."

"I can't do that. I'm a golf god."

Silvia looked at him eyeball to eyeball. "So, what can you do?"

"I don't know. What do you want me to do?"

"You ruined me."

Here, Phor lost whatever momentum he might have established. He grinned. "It was kinda fun though, wasn't it?"

She screamed.

"Sorry. Sorry. I'll make it up to you."

"What does a golf god do?" she asked again.

"I take care of the game of golf. I make sure players honor the game, have fun playing it, that sort of thing."

Silvia raised her chin and with resolute conviction told him, "Then I think you should ruin the game just as you ruined me."

"What?"

"I want you to make all golfers think things will be good, then ruin it for them. You did that to me. Do it to them."

"How?"

"I don't know. I don't play your stupid game."

Phor thought for a moment. He did not want to ruin the game that had become his reason for staying alive as a god, even one as minor as he was. As golf was growing, so was his stature among gods. "You want golfers to think positively and then have something bad happen?"

"Yes."

"If I do that, you'll forgive me?"

She would not give an inch. "If I deem it sufficient."

"I must think about this for a time. May we meet again tomorrow?"

"That can be arranged."

Remember Malcolm Maynard? This is where he came in. That evening his sister told him of her misadventure, crying much of the time but thinking to herself that it had been kinda fun. Malcolm, however, saw a situation that could be to his great advantage. If he could somehow control at least a little of the game he could bet on various outcomes, win an outrageous percentage of the time, and live a life of excessive wealth. He talked Silvia into making a deal with Phor.

The next day, Phor and Silvia met as planned.

"This is what you will do, and I will forgive you. You make sure every golfer is imbued with the optimism that I was, but that this optimism will only rarely be realized."

Phor had to comply. Malcolm got rich betting that players would come up short. The agreement Phor made was that from then on golfers would be sure they will hit the ball far enough but will hit the ball all the way to the hole only the agreed-upon percentage of the time. (The agreed percentage is unknown, but is very low.) Sadly, even though you now know the truth, you are doomed, as we all are, to the same disappointments that to this day plague Sisyphus.

## Why Playing Through a Slower Group Always Results in a Lousy Shot

It doesn't matter if the event occurs on the first tee when the group ahead says it's waiting for one more player, or in the fairway, or on a later tee—the fact is, when one group plays through another, the group playing through will always suffer at least one lousy shot. Most often it will be a topped shot. It won't be a complete whiff, which would still allow a quick re-swing and equally quick exit. It will be a topped shot that requires moving forward only a few feet, getting readjusted, and sometimes even having to go back to the bag to choose a different club.

Those unaware of the power of the golf gods assume it's due to a bit of tension due to extra observing eyes and the unspoken conception that the faster players are good golfers and the slower ones bad golfers, with the added assumption that the slower ones are also less manly.

The problem actually has to do with the belief of Pokkie (the golf god of pace of play) that he can read the thoughts of others. Pokkie has what is called a bicameral mind. Instead of two separate but well-connected brain hemispheres that coordinate functioning like we humans have, he has two hemispheres that are only minimally connected and act almost independently. As with the human brain of thousands of years ago, the voice in one hemisphere seems to come from the outside to the other hemisphere. So, if he were to play though a slow group, his imagination would tell him that his thoughts of the other players' supposed thoughts were actually their statements.

If Pokkie is observing your group go through another, he instills the same so-called ability in you. All your fears and assumptions about the other golfers' possible thoughts become overwhelmingly clear. Anything you think reverberates from you to them to you again and again, until it's lucky you can hold a club, let alone hit the ball.

Naturally, one of the thoughts you might assume they will have is, "Who does this guy think he is, playing through? I hope he screws up." And most often the worst screw-up is the topped shot.

Pokkie, of course, doesn't make this happen. He would like playing through to be more pleasant for everyone. But like an anxious hostess he busies himself to the point where he loses sight of the goal and simply worries the situation into a disaster.

The only good news is that either asking or being asked to play through is such a rare occurrence these days that it is hardly worth worrying about. Pokkie wouldn't think of this, but if you're asked to play through the group ahead of you without your asking, assume that they want to play behind you because they have seen enough of your play to believe that you are by far the superior golfer, and nothing you could do while playing through could change their minds.

On the other hand, if you request to play through and are granted that privilege, assume that the group is so intimidated

*Pokkie*

by either your appearance or your game that they're actually afraid to say "No" and will be afraid to say anything if you screw up.

If you ask to play through and are told "No," the best course of action is to look confused, retreat quietly, and watch each of them top the ball.

# *Why People Yell "Fore" When Their Ball Is About to Hit Someone*

Mary Simpson was ninety-six when she died in 1910. Miss Simpson was a spinster, as they called unmarried ladies in those days, at least ladies who could not be classified as dowagers, an elderly woman of some social standing. Mary, as we shall affectionately call her, was of the lower classes. She was a lady only in bearing and only in her dreams. Prince Charming failed to arrive at her doorstep. Instead, her mother died in childbirth, her father in a mine accident when she was only eleven. Mary was forced to work from the time she was old enough to hold a broom and was expected by a succession of households to wield it like she was born to it. Which, unfortunately, she was.

For almost seventy years she lived under the stairs of stately homes, sweeping, wiping, bowing, serving, polishing, lifting, curtsying, smiling, and weeping. Yet Mary knew that her life was different, better in many ways than that of the high and mighty who attended all the dinners, the hunts, and the fancy dress balls. None of the captains of industry, none of the ladies of the society columns, none of the guests that tramped mud onto the carpets knew of her gift. Mary could see and talk to the spirits.

It wasn't long after her father died that she began talking to him again. Late at night when dogs snore but cats prick up their ears she could see his thin form slowly walking toward her. He would stop ten or fifteen feet away and smile in that wry way he did, sheepishly wave to her, and tell her how sorry he was to have left her. Her friends laughed, so she stopped telling them of his visits. She told her older sister Ida of the meetings, but Ida had such a look on her face that Mary didn't tell her again either.

◆

## *Golf God Factoid*

The average age of the golf gods is 1,851 earth years, excluding the golf god that was formerly a rock.

◆

She didn't see just her father. Over the years, she saw and talked to any number of the spirits of the dead. Among people she considered friends were Joan of Arc, Saint Peter, Richard the Lion Heart, Queen Elizabeth I, and Robin Hood.

However, her name, unknown until now, shall forever be intertwined with golf, for it was her gift that saved a life and exposed for the briefest of moments the great golf god Phor.

Mary was walking along the sea next to the small Kurkotish links course just north of the village itself. It was Saturday afternoon, her usual half day off. The sun encouraged a longer walk than usual; the air was crisp but pure with just enough of a hint of heather to declare it was finally spring.

This day she was pushing a pram cradling the tiny form of her best friend's six-month-old daughter. While the wee one dozed in the sun Mary sat on a bench about ten feet away. She was watching the golfers and the other walkers who were taking advantage of such a fine day.

One player, a rotund older man wearing a bowler hat, was standing at his ball no more than thirty yards away from Mary, ready to swing. He waggled his club back and forth, shifted his feet, and waggled some more. Then he stopped dead, so still he was like a statue. After many moments he took a mighty swing and missed. He began his labored routine of waggles, standing like a statue, swinging again and missing again. By this time Mary was in the daydreaming state that often was rewarded by a visit from her father or another of her long dead friends.

As her eyes took on a faraway gaze she began to see the image of an old man with a full white beard gazing into the pram, looking at the wee Fiona. She wasn't worried. She recognized a spirit when she saw one. His image became more detailed, and she could see he was from another time and another place. "Mary," she whispered as a greeting. The old man looked up at her and smiled. "Phor," he said, softly but with a voice so deep and strong she could feel the vibration in her bones.

Crack. Mary turned at the sound to see that the golfer with the bowler hat had finally struck the ball. It was heading directly at the pram. "Phor!" she yelled at the spirit. The ball was within a yard of smashing into the depths of the pram when Phor easily brushed it aside with a flick of his wrist. All the man who hit the ball could see was a ball about to hit an infant miraculously turning away at the last possible moment.

"Phor," Mary cried again, this time with glee.

The rotund man waddled over to the pram where Mary now stood. "The ball was headed right at the child. How did it miss?"

"You saw the ball. It was deflected by Phor."

"Fore?"

"Aye, Phor."

"I don't understand," the man said.

"He's a god of golf," Mary explained, her gift telling her all she needed to know.

The man shook his head sadly. He had heard about Mary.

Mary had seen that look many times before. "I can tell you don't believe me. But I say to you. Next time you have a ball headed toward a person, you call on Phor and he'll be there for you. He wants no one hurt, right enough."

"Fore."

"That's right, Phor."

"Call out 'fore' if my ball is headed for someone, and it won't hit them?"

"Aye."

So he did that the very next time, and it worked. He told his friends to do it, and it worked for them too. They told their friends and I'm telling you. Next time your ball is headed at someone, yell out his name. It's spelled "Phor." He's always watching out for us. Believe, give him a chance, and he'll be there.

## Anatomy of Golf Disasters

There are two kinds of golf disasters. The rarest are the great disasters such as Sam Snead never winning a U.S. Open. As you know, this was not exactly an accident but it just as well could have been. Much more common are the everyday accidents, almost like fender benders on the freeway. No one really gets hurt, and the damage is eventually forgotten. But always remember that the golf gods are on your side. When a disaster occurs in your game, for the most part it was an accident.

In those rare occurrences when the disaster was not an accident, the golf gods are punishing you for something you did or failed to do, or are using you as an example to teach someone else a lesson, and you just happened to be a good tool for the purpose. You cannot avoid being used as an example unless you are well known and well regarded by the golf gods. You can ensure that you are well known and well regarded by telling each of your playing companions before the round that you are a true believer in the golf gods and that part of your golf god ritual is to buy your playing companions the beverage of their choice after the round. Once they learn of your ritual, they will want to play golf with you all the time and will certainly encourage your devotion to the golf gods.

When a golf disaster is an accident, it truly was not the intent of the golf gods to do you harm. That being said, they suffer no remorse over the results of their folly. Take, for example, the experience of Hiram Hazelwood, a Methodist minister in Farbragh, Massachusetts. He was playing a round of golf at the municipal golf course with his good friend Ronald Fitzgerald, the local high school principal. Both men were highly regarded in the community, honest, forthright, and trusted by young and old. On this particular day the golf gods who were to accompany the good Reverend Hazelwood were Hesta (the golf god of nice things and anything that Phor doesn't get to), Obsissa (the golf god of distance), Pokkie (the golf god of pace of play), and Fabu (the golf god of breaking 100). This quartet was as typical a committee of golf gods as there could be.

On a good day Reverend Hazelwood played in the high eighties to low nineties. The same was true of that day's oppo-

*Obsissa*

nent. The usual wager was beverages at the end of the round, rationalized by both men as being acceptable because they would have bought each other a drink in any event. And most often the drinks were of the softer varieties.

The day was grand. The flags were gently fluffed by a breeze out of the south. The temperature rested in the low seventies. Only a few clouds drifted by during the course of the match. Long drives were common. Pitches ended close to the hole. Difficult putts snaked right, left, then right again before finally falling into the deep end of the bucket. Both men played over their heads, and the match was even going into seventeen. None of this was due to the golf gods. They had yet to form a functioning committee.

As the leading golf god in this group Hesta should have taken command and made things right. However, she was completely uninterested in a match between two men who were so vanilla. Obsissa felt the same. Neither of these golfers had the least interest in swinging hard at the ball. Instead, both seemed content to bunt the ball down the middle and hope for a hard bounce to add distance, which they seemed to be getting. Pokkie was totally content. These two players were moving at a brisk pace, but would allow a Wodehouse Wrecking Crew to plod through just to be polite. As for Fabu and the chance of breaking a hundred, both these golfers habitually did so and were thankful.

In essence, this match was totally out of control, the chances of a golf disaster were extremely high, and neither golfer had a clue.

Reverend Hazelwood had the honor on the seventeenth tee. He hit a beautiful bunt about 190 yards down the right side of the fairway. While placing his ball on a tee, Mister Fitzgerald, who had been out-driven the last four holes, had the fleeting thought that he might clobber the ball twenty paces past his opponent. Obsissa smiled. Now you're talking, he thought. He infused Fitzgerald with a double dose of J. Daly juice. Bam! Fitzgerald swung harder than he had ever swung in his life. The ball took off as if jet-propelled and landed no fewer than fifty yards past Hazelwood's. "Take that, Short Knocker," Fitzgerald said, and instantly regretted his act of bravado toward his good friend. With this, Pokkie became interested. He's always worried about what other people think. In this case he was sure Fitzgerald had totally insulted Hazelwood and took matters into his own hands — or more accurately, put words into Fitzgerald's mouth.

"Sorry to have hit such a good one. Just lucky. Didn't mean anything."

Obsissa, wanting to make sure Hazelwood would want to fight back, whispered into his ear, "Don't get pushed around by a girly man."

This, of course, irritated Hesta. How dare anyone, let alone an underling golf god, use the female gender as a putdown. So she ordered Fabu to make sure Hazelwood had no chance to win and certainly no chance to break 100. She was angry at Obsissa, not Hazelwood, but that didn't matter in the heat of the moment.

Hazelwood, totally innocent and ignoring Obsissa's effort to get him riled up, said in response to his friend's comment, "Ronald, we've had a good match so far, no reason to think that

## *Golf God Factoid*

Golf god Sarah Winston played a bit part in the movie
*Caddyshack*.

won't continue. I will match your good shots with good shots of
my own, and let the better man win." Oh, little did the man of
God know.

Since Reverend Hazelwood was on track to shoot about 88,
Fabu had to add at least twelve strokes to his score in the last two
holes to please Hesta, who could make big trouble if he didn't.
The difficulty was that number seventeen was a short par 4, and
so was eighteen. Neither had any trouble to speak of, no lakes,
out-of-bounds, major bunkers, anything that could contribute
to a disaster. Fabu had to be creative, with Hesta looking on.

Hazelwood dead topped the ball with his second swing. And
he repeated this on swings three, four, and five. His topped fifth
shot rolled near the green, where he proceeded to four-putt for
a quintuple bogey and thus to be one down in the match. "That
was certainly a surprise," he said, somewhat dazed.

The two trudged up the hill to the eighteenth tee. At Obsissa's urging, Fitzgerald blasted his drive down the middle with a
roundhouse swing. With Fabu's intervention, Hazelwood swung
once and missed, then sliced the ball into the long rough about
a hundred yards off the tee. Both men began walking over to
where the ball should have been. Hazelwood waved off Fitzgerald. "I have it spotted. You go up to your ball. I'll be fine." Fabu
was about to "help" again.

As Fitzgerald walked to his ball, Hazelwood cried, "I have
it!" and commenced to hit his next shot back to the fairway.
Both players had a tough time, taking four to reach the green.
Fitzgerald was away and stroked his putt to within eight feet
of the hole. He was laying five. Hazelwood hit his putt into the
heart of the cup to win the hole and tie the match. Shaking his
head, Fitzgerald went to pick his friend's ball from the cup.

"Weren't you playing a Dunlop 2?" he asked.

"Yes, I was."

"This is a Dunlop 3," came the cold statement of fact from Fitzgerald.

"Then I must have been playing a Dunlop 3 and made a mistake."

"You played a 2 from the tee. I saw the number on the ball. You must have switched balls in the rough."

"Are you calling me a cheat?"

"If you cheat, that's what you get called."

"No one calls me a cheat."

That's when Hazelton said something in Latin to Fitzgerald, and Obsissa, enjoying the heck out of the situation, urged Fitzgerald to use hand gestures suggesting to Hazelwood what he could do with his ball, upon which Hazelwood tried to use his putter to perform an act that is illegal in about half the South-

*Fabu*

ern states, which prompted the horrified golf professional to rush half a dozen caddies to intervene while he called the police, which, of course, resulted in a local reporter rushing over so an article could be written for the morning paper describing the scene with somewhat embellished details so that the townspeople had a totally incorrect impression of what happened, which still didn't stop them from ruining the careers of both men.

By this time, all four golf gods were busy doing other things.

# Why Golfers Get Bad Bounces

Logically, over time, good bounces should equal bad bounces, but it doesn't seem to work that way. In every golfer's mind a good bounce is way overdue and a bad bounce is unfair.

To understand this phenomenon we have to delve a little into existential philosophy. This approach maintains that life has no meaning. Golfers can easily and wholeheartedly accept this concept after a triple bogey or two. If life has no meaning, you have two options, give up or create meaning. This thought leads to the basic tenet of existentialism, *existence precedes essence*. Translated from the Latin, this means that you have to be alive before you can get anything done.

Hence, once you have decided to play golf it is up to you to figure out what it means.

Jean-Paul Sartre, a twenty handicapper from Paris, France, gives us some help in making sense of the game. He actually wrote a number of books and stage plays that try to explain golf. The most famous is probably his *No Exit*, unfortunately written in French but supposedly about how once you get hooked on golf it's difficult to give up the game. However, he did write an article for his local golf league newsletter that has been translated into English.

*No Fair*, written in 1955, is about good and bad bounces. His theme in this long article is that the golfer must make sense of the golf experience to find meaning in it, for otherwise it would be like a walk through a park with a stone in your shoe. He begins by stating that without movement, there is not life; therefore, the golfer essentially creates life* by creating movement in the golf ball. Once this *existence* is created *essence* must be found. Obviously, the golfer must create *essence* by finding meaning in where the ball ends up. Sartre concludes by saying that the golfer, *who has created life*, must, like God, take responsibility for defining good and evil.

---

* "Life" in this sense can be a number of things including an extension of the golfer's existence or of potential being placed in the golf ball.

It should be clear even to the most casual reader that the golfer has the responsibility to judge good and evil every time he or she has created existence, that is, hit the golf ball.

But the question remains: Why does it appear that many more bad bounces occur than good ones?

Nothing could be simpler to answer.

Every time the golfer hits the ball and creates *existence*, *essence* must follow. Since the golfer's intention is for good, it is completely up to the golfer to declare when good has occurred or when bad has happened. Furthermore, logic dictates that "good" must be clearly good, while "bad" can be bad or maybe just "not good." Thus, a ball lying in the fairway some distance away could still be "bad" when it is in a divot, covered with mud, or "sitting down." Over time, a golfer learns not to declare a shot "good" until *existence*, that is, movement, has ceased. Others can say "good shot" while the ball is in the air, but the one who created *existence* must be careful when defining *essence*.

You can test this phenomenon by making observations on almost any green. Many times a player will mishit a putt, declare it to be terrible, yet the ball ends up going in the hole. Rarely, if ever, will you hear someone describe a shot as good until the ball has stopped and its *essence* has been closely examined.

It is for these reasons that golfers will declare a bounce bad even while the ball still has existence. Thus bad is declared even if good can still happen. But only rarely will the golfer deem that a positive essence has been achieved until existence has expired. Thus, bad bounces are recognized and counted many, many times, whereas good bounces are ignored and forgotten as soon as the next quest to create existence occurs.

## *Golf God Factoid*

Golf gods travel from place to place without conscious thought. They just are at the place they want to be. The same is true for other things they want. For example, a glass of iced tea will appear in the golf god's hand halfway on its travel to the mouth.

For the most part the golf gods are not involved in bad bounces. The golf gods understand how the universe works. They know that randomness is the optimal and true form of fair, and they want to protect that element of golf as much as possible. (They are losing ground in this effort.) They are providing the fairest test of skill on the planet. They are aware, however, of the awesome responsibilities of existence and essence and wish us beginners in this realm well.

# Why Some People Insist That Golf Be Like Every Other Sport

If you read the sports pages of your local paper, there is no doubt that at one time or another in the past four years you have come across writings criticizing golf for not being like other sports. The authors of letters to the editor bemoan that golf is backward, silly, archaistic, sissified, hypocritical, outdated, unappealing, and on and on and on. The thrust of these statements (they really can't be dignified as being arguments since most seem to be made by potbellied middle-aged men whose last contact with sport was as a fourth-string tackle on the high school football team) is that golf is a nonsensical activity since it is not a sport, does not allow fans to abandon common sense and decency, and expects players to remain gentlemen and ladies no matter what agonies are being suffered. A further jab at golf is that even at the professional level some yahoo watching on television a thousand miles away can call a penalty on a player, causing all sorts of havoc up to and including the player's disqualification.

Is golf a sport? It is not. A sport demands enough exertion to require a postgame shower. If you don't have to shower after doing it, it's not a sport. A sport also requires a uniform. A person can dress for golf and walk down any street, and no one would notice. Sports also put players at some physical risk, like having a ball thrown at you at a hundred miles an hour or being cut down at the knees by a 300-pound smelly guy. A golfer's sore back or hurt wrist is as much a sports injury as gardener's thumb. To say golf is a sport because it requires hand-eye coordination is to call driving a car to the minimart a sport for the same reason. The only semi-legitimate reason to call golf a sport comes from the common sports practice of wearing a favorite athlete's jersey and number. A golf fan can do something similar by going to a pro shop and buying a golf shirt or sweater with a favorite player's advertiser's logo on it.

A real sport doesn't allow you to pause and enjoy a refreshing drink whenever you like, either. Or drive a little mini-car from activity point to activity point. The fields of sports battles don't have flower gardens spread all around and full-grown trees to add depth and character to the surroundings, or attractive water features that catch the eye. Real sports require such intense concentration that players cannot be counted on to call penalties or errors. Specialists must be hired to do the job.

Golf fans cannot be true sports fans either. Golf fans do not come to an arena, a closed-in place to sit and see all the action. They have to hike over hill and dale to see what is going on, and even then see very little. They are required to give up cameras and cell phones. They have to be quiet if they're going to be allowed to watch the action. They are not supposed to root against anybody. For players and fans both, golf simply isn't a sport.

Yet, some people demean it because it isn't one. What exactly do they want and why?

What they want is brutality, for the participants and the fans. Sport is one person or one team beating the daylights out of another in every sense of the word. Golf, where the primary opponent is the course and the other opponent is yourself, doesn't make sense to the sport-obsessed mind. For such a mind somebody has to be dominated, somebody bloodied, somebody made very much the worse for wear. To this testosterone-engorged sports brain, fans also have to be made rabid, identifying with those in battle to a degree that they too are fighting the enemy.

Why do they want golf to be the same as other sports? Unfortunately, this is due to a miscalculation by the golf gods.

During the latter stages of the U.S.–Soviet Cold War the golf gods decided that the world needed to focus on the most gentlemanly of activities, namely golf. They set up and groomed a player who would become so popular that even the occupant of the White House would be better known for golf than for waging war. The golf gods hoped that this would be the start of the world becoming more civilized. They wanted a common man, someone everyone could identify with. Arnold Palmer was promoted in order to woo the world to the exciting but still gentlemanly game of golf. Insofar as this was concerned the effort was a big success. Where it backfired was that Arnie had a slashing, attacking style. The golf gods thought that he was young and would develop a smoother style as he matured. Little did they realize this broad-shouldered steel driver of a man would just slash harder as he got older, suggesting not a movement toward world peace but that golf might soon become a real sport.

Weekend golfers mimicked his style. Professional players became hitters instead of swingers. The power game proudly flexed its biceps.

At the same time watering golf courses became more common. This meant that flying the ball to the target was more effective than running the ball along the ground. Approach shots mimicked mortars fired at the green. Gentle bump-and-runs were replaced by the more aggressive sticking the ball and sucking it back.

It doesn't take a genius to see that golf has been edging toward "sports" in the last few decades. Sports fans who observe golf get a whiff of what it could be and urge it to become that. Golfers, at the same time, are doing the same. Distance is replacing accuracy in importance. Muscle power is replacing technique in the repertoire of many players. Domination is overcoming honor during competition. When a putt drops a fist pump has replaced a thankful wave.

## *Golf God Factoid*

Hesta, in her human guise, is a member of Augusta National.

It used to be that a player would adjust to the demands of golf. Today, players are clamoring for reform—modernize the old goat, they cry. The golf gods are concerned but are unsure what to do. If you have some ideas about golf becoming like common sports and what can be done about it, let them know. All you have to do is think of any of the golf gods and offer your suggestion just loud enough to be heard at least three feet away. One of them will hear you, and all will be grateful. They will also reward you handsomely.

They groomed Arnold Palmer to promote world peace. The world is worse off now than when they started. Arnold Palmer has given golf and the world a vast amount of goodwill, but asking him to create world peace was asking too much. The golf gods realize this now and are sorry.

# Why New Clubs Work Better Than Your Old Ones for Three Rounds

You bought a new driver or even a whole new set. You did this because you tried someone's driver or iron and hit the bejesus out of the ball, or you saw an ad and decided to believe the hype. In either event, you are attempting to buy a better golf game. Think about this for a moment. You are attempting to buy a better golf game. Put that concept together with the fact that there are golf gods. See the problem here?

If you're not sure of the problem, here it is. Golf is a game so special, so fundamental to the functioning of the universe, that it has gods to watch over it. Do you believe, in any possible way, that these gods would think it was appropriate to commercialize the game, to make it something you could buy off the shelf? Or do you think that the golf gods want you to respect the game, to dedicate yourself to it, to invest your sweat, yea even your blood? Get the idea now?

So, you may ask, why do new clubs work well at all? Good question. Here's the answer. If you are so dumb as to think you should desecrate the game by attempting to buy a better one, you need to be taught a lesson. You try a club, hit it better than your old one, you think for a nanosecond, then buy the new club, paying a great deal of money. If it failed to perform right away you'd think it was just a bad choice of club. You made a purchase decision based on a fluke or too little data. You'd be off the hook. However, if the new clubs perform for at least an entire round or maybe two or even better three, then the clubs work fine, and it's you who are the problem. By setting up the universe to work this way the golf gods are hoping that you'll sooner or later get the idea that it's not the club, it's you.

The golf gods are so much on our side it's sad to see how little we appreciate them. Next time you play your old set, say thanks out loud to one or more of your favorite golf gods, and if you buy a new set before your current one is worn out, watch out. Accepting the gift of a new set is okay as long as you give your old set to someone needy or to a charitable organization.

Do not leave it to rot hidden somewhere, gathering dust and mold and mice droppings in the garage or the attic.

---

## *Golf God Factoid*

The average vacation for a golf god is only two weeks per year. However, there are 63 golf god holidays available. On days off, most take human form and spend time in Kennebunkport, Maine, or in Tuscany. Four golf gods swear by Myrtle Beach, while a group takes semi-annual trips to Bandon, Oregon. One actually climbed Mount Everest, while another spends time off working as a cab driver in Pakistan.

---

## *Why Golfers Talk to Their Golf Balls*

You've heard it—"Get up!" and "Go left" and "Don't go there!" and a hundred other things. "Grow Teeth" is probably the most descriptive. You've probably yelled at or coaxed your ball yourself. We all know the ball doesn't listen. A golf ball cannot listen. We know that but yet we talk to them.

There can be only two reasons for this behavior. One is that at one time the ball actually could and did listen, and our behavior is a throwback to this time. The other is that even if balls cannot and do not listen, somehow talking to the golf ball actually does some good. The fact is that both of these possibilities are valid.

Although it may seem chauvinistic and a gross generalization to say so, the first reason why golfers talk to their golf balls was completely the fault of the typical femaleness of Hesta and Sarah Winston. These two female golf gods got to chatting over tea and crumpets one afternoon and decided that there wasn't enough talking going on during the typical golf game. They thought that over a three-hour round (as they were in those halcyon days), there should be much more social congress. (That's what they said, "social congress.") To accomplish that it seemed like a good idea to have golf balls respond, not totally, but somewhat, to the exhortations of the golfers. What they hoped would happen was that a golfer would say something like, "Go right, go right," and the ball oft-times would go right. When the ball went right, the golf gods figured that would be cause for "social congress." On the occasions that the ball didn't go right, that also would stimulate "social congress" as to why the ball didn't go right this particular time.

And in actual fact this is what happened. For about a two-month period golf balls responded much of the time, to some degree, to the cries of the golfer who hit the ball. (This was after some fine-tuning, since initially balls would curve and swoop in the air all over the place responding to whatever calls they heard from anywhere.)

Hesta and Ms. Winston were pleased with the experiment and were discussing it over another afternoon's tea (again with crumpets). It was Hesta who remarked, "Trouble is, it's not really golf anymore, is it?" They both agreed it was not. Then she said, "And it really isn't social congress either, is it, talking to the golf ball." And both agreed it wasn't. She also remarked, "And the increase in subsequent discussion amongst the golfers isn't really occurring in any meaningful way, is it?" They both agreed to this statement as well. Finally she concluded, "Let's stop this." So they did. But golfers keep talking. You never know when the golf gods may change their minds.

The second concept, that talking to an unresponsive golf ball actually does some good, has to do with a human drive called "avoiding looking like an idiot." It's a subtle psychological phenomenon but easy to understand. Talking to the ball is not intended to affect ball flight, but to protect self-esteem. Say you just hit your ball way right. You know you screwed up. To save face you need to let others know that you know that you screwed up. So immediately upon knowing you screwed up you yell at the ball to go left, alerting everyone that you know exactly where the ball should go, even though, somehow, probably through some fluke, your swing didn't get it going in the right direction.

Thus, by talking to the ball, you're demonstrating your vast knowledge of golf, declaring that your swing is much more consistent and good than what has just occurred, expressing with confidence the exact degree of waywardness of the ball and defining what the outcome should have been under normal circumstances. It is mostly men who employ this limp, face-saving device.

# Why Golfers Wear Ridiculous Clothes

In the olden days golfers could be expected to wear coats and ties while on the links. At least you could expect gentlemen players to do that. Some members of clubs even had uniforms that were the required attire while on the course. Ladies were also expected to play dressed up for the occasion. The riff-raff who played golf dressed in the clothes they wore for everything from works day to Sunday services. Professional players wore white shirts and ties into the 1930s. At this point, subtle changes began to take place. Golfers found clothes to wear that were comfortable, like the T-shirts that replaced more restrictive dress shirts. Pants remained stylishly loose. Pleats hid a lot of faults.

If you looked at a series of photographs from 1950 through 1965 you'd notice that in 1961 things changed. In 1960 most players wore plain colored pants and equally plain knit shirts. Women wore skirts and sleeveless blouses. Plaid pants appeared almost overnight in 1961.

This is how it happened.

In 1959 Mike Sywicki enjoyed his best bowling season ever. The Hamtramck Ravens came in second in their General Motors summer recreation league. Mike loved his bowling. That Christmas Mrs. Sywicki, in an attempt to "class up" her husband, bought him a set of Sam Snead autograph golf clubs. She wheeled out the clubs, a bag, and a pull cart.

"What the hell are these?" he asked that Christmas morn.

"They're golf clubs," his wife replied.

"What the hell am I going to do with golf clubs?"

"They're golf clubs. You play golf with them."

"Why the hell would I play golf?"

"You'll like the game."

Mike's education as a golfer went on for some time that morning. To keep the peace, he went out one Saturday morning in spring to the local muni and played nine holes. He hated every second. Complaining to his friends at the GM plant that Monday, he learned that other wives had given the same Christmas gift. A light bulb went on. Mike is no dummy, and neither are his friends. Recognizing a men's beer drinking opportunity when it presented itself, they agreed to meet the next Saturday morning. The second time out wasn't so bad. They played nine holes and then sat in the bar watching the Tigers game the rest of the afternoon. This was repeated every Saturday until Labor Day. By the time the next summer arrived they were ready to join the GM after-work nine-hole league.

Mike and his friends were just regular guys. They didn't notice much beyond themselves on the course and didn't watch any of the limited golf that was on television. They didn't read the couple of golf magazines that were around. Basically they were bowlers who played in a golf summer league. Their chosen attire for golf was, naturally enough, bowling shirts. They didn't notice what others wore and didn't notice that others noticed what they wore.

Mike's wife noticed. "You're not wearing that, are you?"

"Hey, I'm going to play golf, what's it to you?"

Mike's friend Butch got a pair of pants with the images of the new General Motors cars stenciled on them. It was a novelty item to promote the new line. He wore them during the league's next match.

"Snazzy threads, there, Butch."

"Ain't they great? I can get you a pair, cheap."

Since Mike was now playing golf once a week his wife decided to "class" him up a bit more. Knowing that golf is a Scottish game she went to a Scottish store and bought her husband plaid pants. She wanted to get him a kilt but thought better of it.

"Snazzy threads, there, Mike."

"Ain't they great? I can get you a pair, cheap."

All that summer in Hamtramck the boys would try to outdo one another. When one wore plaid the other wore brighter plaid. When one wore pleated slacks the other wore ones without. Black shoes were exchanged for white. Tops went from bowling shirts to solid color Ban-Lon, to multi-colored cable-knits, to images of flamingos.

Unfortunately, these golfers from this small suburb of Detroit went on buddy vacations and took their clubs and their clothes. Combine men on their own, four hours or more of showing off, beer and conversation, and lack of female constraints, and you have a fashion disaster on your hands. That disaster began in 1959 and exploded worldwide in 1961. American Ryder Cup players seem bent on continuing this tradition.

The golf gods wanted you to know that they had nothing to do with this phenomenon.

### *Golf God Factoid*

The majority of golf gods own pets. Dogs are most popular, golden retrievers being the favorite breed. Cats are a close second with no specific kind standing out. One golf god has a turtle. One has a parrot. One has a rhinoceros named Tootsie.

# Why Tiger Woods Changes His Swing

In 1997, against the best golfers in the world, Tiger Woods won the Masters Golf Championship by twelve strokes. In 2000, against the best golfers in the world, he won the U.S. Open by fifteen strokes. This amounts to scoring almost four strokes better than anyone else for each eighteen-hole round. In between, in tournament after tournament, he humbled fellow competitors with every facet of his game. He had arguably become the best golfer in the history of the game, dominating his contemporaries as no other player had ever done. Johnny Miller described Tiger Woods's swing in 2000 as "perfect." Yet Tiger left Hank Haney, the instructor who had helped him reach this pinnacle, for other teachers to make him even better. Why mess with such success? According to Bok, the golf god of the swing, this is why Tiger continually tweaks his swing.

The answer goes back in time, back to when Tiger's father Earl was serving in Vietnam. Earl was an educated man, a thoughtful man, a man of grace and dignity. Unlike other soldiers who took their R & R (rest and relaxation) on the Ginza in Tokyo in search of booze and broads, Earl would visit museums, art galleries, and manufacturing plants. At the Toyota factory he was introduced to lean production methods. He marveled at how much quality could be put into automobiles. He mentioned to one worker, "Top quality, eh?" The worker responded with the only word he knew in English, "Perfection."

On subsequent R & R visits, Earl went only to the Toyota plant. He learned the idea of constant small improvements: small improvements, but improvements that were aimed at eventual perfection. He vowed that if he ever had the chance to raise a child his way, he would help his son work toward perfection one small step at a time. This child he would name Toyota.

Things didn't work out quite like Earl had thought. He named his last born Tiger in honor of a fallen comrade but kept the idea of perfection. Small step by small step Tiger grew from a skinny little kid into a skinny tall adult who keeps getting bigger and better.

---

## *Golf God Factoid*

There are two ways to discover if a golf god has assumed human form and is nearby. One is to see if the "person" smells faintly of pumpkin and paprika. The other is to simply ask. They will tell you outright if they are a golf god.

---

Most golf fans know that Tiger is driven to overtake Jack Nicklaus's eighteen professional major wins total. Tiger also wants to win the Grand Slam. For a while he did hold all four major titles, which he subjectively decided was a grand slam, but he hadn't accomplished the real feat of winning the Masters, the U.S. Open, the British Open, and the American PGA in a calendar year. This, however, is not his real goal. Had this been his primary goal he would have kept the swing that was so astoundingly successful in the 1990s and early 2000s. He is after much more.

His friendly rival, LPGA golfer Annika Sorenstam, thinks she knows. They needle one another about major wins and the attempt to win the Grand Slam on their respective tours. But underlying this public rivalry is a concept driven into Annika by the Swedish Golf Federation. A perfect round of golf is a 54, with a birdie every hole. Annika has a 59 in competition and wants to be the first to scale the heights of a 54. She knows Woods has a better chance, but she doesn't know what golf god Bok knows.

Tiger isn't interested in a mere 54. A birdie on every hole isn't perfection to him. Tiger will continue to work on his swing, risking losing it, in his quest to shoot a 50 in competition. With his distance, par 5s become par 4s. He intends to eagle the par 5s and birdie the rest to shoot a 50.

There's more.

He also figures that one or two par 4s might be drivable and also open for eagles. Tiger wants to shoot a 50, but in his heart of hearts his actual goal is to shoot either 49 or, with luck, a 48. At that point, he will retire.

Until Tiger reaches his real goal, you can bet that he will be working on improving his swing.

The golf gods have not been clear as to whether Tiger will accomplish this nearly impossible feat. They have not indicated whether he will do it on his own or with their help. I would not bet against Tiger shooting a 49 on the PGA Tour within the next two years.

# The Golf Gods

This is where the clubface hits the ball, so to speak. You are about to learn some simple details about each of the golf gods. They are not presenting these brief histories for their own aggrandizement but totally for your benefit. You have a chance to play better golf than you ever imagined and to enjoy every round at almost illegal levels of delight. Remember the first time you successfully sneaked a cookie from the cookie jar, drove a car by yourself, discovered the opposite sex? This could be better than that.

Here's the deal. The golf gods have always been there for your game, and you've had some primitive awareness of their impact. You've heard them mentioned, maybe even talked about them yourself, but you did so without what Phor would call true knowledge. What you said was just words, meaningless and without form or adequate appreciation. You are now going to crunch into the apple of knowledge, take a big bite out of ignorance, and chomp on the idiocy of superstition.

Let's begin with an overview.

Like all deities the golf gods have powers that ebb and flow with the number and intensity of believers. The golf gods are vastly underpowered compared to the world's major religions such as Christianity, which has an estimated 2.1 billion believers, and Islam, with 1.3 billion. Hinduism at 900 million and Buddhism at 480 million also leave the golf gods in the dust. If we assume that only a third of golfers are true believers in the golf gods, then golf god believers number about 18 million. That puts golf ahead of Judaism, Baha'i, Jainism, Shinto, Cao Dai, Zoroastrianism, Tenrikyo, Neo-Paganism, Unitarian-Universalism, Rastafarianism, and Scientology.

Unfortunately, this does not mean the golf gods have greater power than any other religion. The golf gods are spirits, very much below religion and only somewhat elevated above astrology. Unlike a religion in which you can do the prescribed things and find salvation, you can do exactly right by a golf god and receive nothing, or in some cases find yourself worse off.

It's a complicated situation. Remember that when you play a round of golf there is a committee of golf gods assigned to your play. In a foursome that means the attention of sixteen golf gods for the group (although one or more golf gods may be on more than one committee within the foursome), plus any individual golf gods who may show up. If you're the only believer in the group you'll be fine; the golf gods will look favorably on you. The same holds true if you and a friend are playing against the other two, even if your friend hasn't yet learned the truth about the golf gods (but it would be to your advantage to clue him/her in). However, if both sides have the same number of believers, the side that acknowledges the golf gods the most during play usually will curry the most favor, all else being equal, which is rarely the case.

Overall, stay calm, drink plenty of fluids, think about the golf gods before beginning every hole, keep the faith, and know as much about each golf god as you can. The idea is to keep your relationship fresh with the golf gods. Don't repeat the same old requests and supplications. They are profoundly intelligent and easily insulted. Be creative in your relationship. Make each hole a new date with the golf gods. Don't fear them. Enjoy them. They want to be your friends, not your stooges or servants.

# *The Five Golf God Commandments*

These five commandments were created over a golf god weekend retreat five years ago to help players understand how best to relate to the golf gods. Like all commandments you can choose to follow them totally, somewhat, or not at all. Guess which way would provide you the most benefit. There are only five; how tough can it be?

## *Choose a guardian golf god*

Each season you must choose a guardian golf god, the one golf god who will be the primary golf god for you all season and the guardian golf god you will call on first to get control of your committee. Once you choose your guardian golf god, that golf god will make sure you and your game are taken care of. Call on your guardian golf god if problems arise, explain the situation and what you want, and if at all possible your guardian golf god will make it right.

The length of a "season" is up to you. It can be a playing season for those who have one, an entire calendar year, or like a fiscal year—any span of at least nine months but not more than twelve. You can have no more than two guardian golf gods within any consecutive twelve months. You can choose the same guardian golf god as many time times as you wish.

You have only three specific obligations regarding your guardian golf god:

- Choose one as described above
- Write your guardian golf god's name on your scorecard every time you play
- Make a charitable contribution in the name of your guardian golf god on your guardian golf god's honorary birthday (you can choose the date—many players make it their own birth date for easy remembering).

Read the golf god descriptions and think over your options, then choose your guardian golf god for the season. Here's some inside information: many, many golfers seem to choose Hesta, almost four to one in comparison to choosing Phor or any of the other golf gods.

## *Do not speak ignorantly of the golf gods*

This is why the book was written. The golf gods tired of hearing the masses exclaiming, "The golf gods were _____ (fill in the blank)." Can anyone presume to know what a golf god is thinking or feeling? Of course not, but they hear golfers all over the world make one inane comment after another, twenty-four hours a day, seven days a week, fifty-two weeks a year and they demand that it stops.

Here are the rules. Say what you want to your guardian golf god, when you want. You can be frustrated, livid, thankful, or anything else. You can feel and think anything, and you can say what you want to say directly to your guardian golf god. That is okay. You can do the same with whomever you guess is on your golf god committee. If you complain to a golf god who is not on your committee you will be forgiven automatically. No worries there. You can complain, but do not assume and do not accuse.

You are forbidden to assume you know what any golf god is thinking. You can guess all you want, but you are not allowed to say a sentence beginning with "The golf gods . . ." and finishing with a conclusion of what they are thinking or feeling. One reason is that you will be wrong. Any time you use the plural "golf gods" for what they may be about collectively you'll be wrong. They never think, feel, or do anything collectively. There is always some difference, however slight. The other reason is that they hate it—probably the only time they feel the same way about anything.

Naturally, if you say ill things about the golf gods, you should expect a quick retirement from the game, but only after appropriate suffering.

## *Honor the golf gods by holding the game above almost all other pastimes*

You have to realize that the golf gods have put a lot of emotional investment into golf. Many could have been gods of other activities, but they chose golf. Try to remember that golf is the reason they exist. Be that as it may, they also appreciate the enjoyment of lovemaking, cutting into a thick, juicy steak, or cementing a lucrative business deal. What they expect, what they demand, is that while on the golf course you pay attention to golf and little else. They don't mind you doing a little business here and there or trying to impress a date, but you put yourself in peril if you do too much other than concentrating on your game.

You are asking for trouble if your cell phone rings on the course, and in more trouble if you answer it. If you leave your loved one naked and needy in bed to go play golf, the golf gods may wonder at your sanity but will applaud your dedication, to a point. Leave your lover lacking too often and they will think you're obsessed, something no god wants of any believer.

It won't be easy, but you have to please the golf gods by placing golf exactly where it should be in your life. Watch for signs; they'll tell you when it's too much or too little.

## *You must keep your golf day sacred*

The golf gods don't want to usurp religion. They certainly don't want to be worshipped. Think about it, though. Until this book was put together, everyone talked about the golf gods, made things up about them that were not based on any facts, even as they have worked hard to take good care of our game for going on two hundred years. They want to be respected, and they want the game to be respected. They also want to team with all golfers everywhere to protect and enhance our great game. Following are a few suggestions.

| Dos | Don'ts |
|---|---|
| Arrive in time to get unhurriedly prepared. | Wear anything that exposes more body hair than the amount of hair you have on your head. |
| Thank those who help you. | |
| Minimize your divot pattern on the range. | Take a divot on your practice swing. |
| Drive the speed limit getting to the course. | Show up late for your tee time. |
| Make wagers that are within everyone's comfort zone. | Swear unless absolutely necessary to prevent apoplexy. |
| Mark your ball on the green correctly. | Cheat, ever, ever, ever. |
| Walk whenever you can. | Yell every time something the least bit interesting happens. |
| Minimize logo wear. | |

The golf gods want you to carve out your golf time as something significant in your life. It is not to be half-hearted or haphazard. They want your approach to golf to be thoughtful. Before you leave the house make sure you have enough balls and tees, a ball repair tool, and ball markers. Make sure you have sunscreen and a towel. Kiss the spouse and kids. Let them know when you'll be home.

Just like you, the golf gods look forward to a good golf game. Don't disappoint them. Don't be sloppy. Honor the game, those who play it, and those who watch over it.

## *Make two sacrifices for the golf gods per season*

Nothing could be easier to fulfill than this commandment. The golf gods want to make sure there is balance in your life and to ensure that they are not the be-all, end-all, do-all center of your life. All you have to do is knowingly sacrifice something golfy for something nongolfy twice a year to demonstrate that you are not obsessed with golf. For example, you could tell your wife that you will not play golf next weekend in order to take her to the opera and to dinner afterwards. However, this would not count if you didn't plan on playing or if something came up so you couldn't play anyway. It has to be a sacrifice.

Buying your wife a surprise gift for no reason at all instead of a new 5-wood would be a good sacrifice, as would the golfing wife giving up the opera and dinner afterward to allow her husband to play thirty-six holes. Two sacrifices. That's all they expect, a simple sacrifice two times in a year. It will do you good.

You can gain favor by making more sacrifices, but do so only in multiples of nine. Somehow this has some significance to them.

These are the five golf god commandments. You are probably already doing most of them because they're the right things to do. But now you know why to do them. They are what the golf gods want you to do to contribute to the game, to honor them, and to maximize the joy and contentment of your golfing life. You may never again see commandments that fit so well into your values, proof again that the golf gods are behind you 100 percent.

# *Golf God Histories*

Each golf god is described in these aspects: area of responsibility, golf god level, a short biography, what the golf god wants, how to become that golf god's friend, and a pledge as to what that golf god will offer if chosen as your guardian golf god, plus a selection of those mortals who currently have that golf god as a guardian or in the past chose that golf god as their golf god guardian.

Keep the commandments in mind as you go through the descriptions of the golf gods. You'll want to choose your guardian golf god with care. You can also gain benefit by finding a description of a minor god that may be affecting your game, like Chit, the golf god of bunkers who is described in the Minor Golf Gods section. Phor, of course, comes first, followed by Hesta as the two Super Major Golf Gods.

You might read just one description and then go play using what you learned to see how it works. If you have success, then read about another golf god and do the same thing. If you don't have success with the first golf god you learn about, either reread the description and try again, or, if you want to take a chance, read about a different golf god and try out what you learned about that one. It could be that the first golf god hasn't been assigned to your committees or that he/she/it wasn't paying attention to your call for some reason.

If you come in contact with someone who has had a particular golf god as a guardian, don't hesitate to ask how it worked for them.

In any event, take it slow, learn by doing, and don't worry about a thing. Your intentions mean a lot.

# The Super Major Golf Gods

## *Phor and Hesta*

Phor was the first golf god and is the supreme golf god. Hesta was the second golf god. Although they are not married, they are considered a couple. Even so, the relationship is loosely enough defined that they can often go years without being together or even talking with each other. They have great affection for one another, and everyone assumes that soon enough they will marry.

Phor has many human traits. He can easily be swayed by a womanly smile or a sidelong glance, something that Hesta uses to great advantage, but which also causes her significant heartache when used by others. Phor can blow hot or cold, while Hesta is like a fragrant Hawaiian breeze.

The thing to keep in mind is that Phor's existence is golf. No entity in history is more connected to the game, every facet of the game, than Phor. He owes his existence to golf and treats it as a sacred trust.

Hesta, on the other hand, had many options for her life yet has learned to make golf her top priority. She, maybe more than Phor, understands and appreciates the sweet agony of our game.

Both want your help to make golf the game that lasts 10,000 years.

# Phor

*Area of Responsibility*

All of Golf

*Golf God Level*

Super Major

*Biography*

Although he would love to be able to trace his linage to Dievas, a major god of the Baltic region, or to his second in command, Perkunas, the god of thunder, Phor (ancient name: Shega) was actually the youngest son of a second cousin of Perkunas. Any meaningful relationship to the well-known spirits of that region would be a stretch. Be that as it may, in his ancient role Phor had responsibilities and worshippers.

Even though he was not of the first rank, these responsibilities were significant. In these ancient days much of a god's time was spent either quarrelling or actually fighting with other gods. Phor's distant relative Perkunas was in constant battle with Velnias, ruler of the underworld. Helping Perkunas was the blacksmith god, Teliavelis, who had crafted the sun among other accomplishments. Helping Teliavelis help Perkunas was Phor's job in his earlier incarnation as Shega.

Phor's responsibilities were twofold. To help the good-guy gods he was to sound the alarm whenever Velnias or his henchmen rose from the underworld and traveled among the living. This was not easy to do since they were very crafty and had thousands of disguises from which to choose. The only clue to their accession was that within a fifty-mile radius dogs tended to turn around three times before lying down rather than their usual two—that and a very slight odor of sulfur.

The other responsibility Phor had was to the people. They were poor farmers and depended on their gods for a good harvest and comfort during their cruel winters. Again, Phor was not a significant god making or breaking the harvest or keeping the wolves from the door, but he was important, important in the way parking on the correct side of the gas pump is important. Phor's job with the people was to ward off the last straw, the small insult or injury that would finally overwhelm a good-hearted, hardworking peasant. He was called Shega because that was the native word for "little favor."

For over a thousand years Phor kept his post protecting the more important gods and the people with equal effort and with good success. Only once did the evil from the underground manage to pass him undetected. Within hours of their turning all the rivers into carbolic acid he sounded the alarm, and the only damage was that a few lawns that were watered that day turned an ugly brown.

Phor was proud that he never let any people down. He successfully kept more than four trillion small insults and hurts from metastasizing. Countless men and women had a chance to overcome daily strife, to raise happy families, to enjoy bits and pieces of contentment during their short, difficult lives. Many on their deathbeds remembered to thank Phor, and for that he was a happy god.

Phor was a good god during his time. He was adored by the people and had earned their love and respect by his intentions and his deeds. Like any competent living entity, he learned as he worked. He learned of the importance of trying hard, of doing the right thing, of contributing to the welfare of others, and the value of the struggle, win or lose.

Then the Christians came. Conversion was delayed in this region compared to other areas such as Zemaitija, the western region of Lithuania, which began its conversion back in 1413. Yet the onslaught was constant and merciless. Over the next four hundred years, the people had other spiritual resources, ones who promised miracles. They began to forget Phor's little favors, and soon enough they began to forget him. By the time he heard the call from Scotland only a handful of people even knew who he was, and they really couldn't be called true believers. Their families had traditions, only traditions, no longer devotion. Phor's days were numbered.

It was a gift to learn of the game of golf, the microcosm of life in a few hours' walk in a park. He again was able to contribute to the well-being of others in a most important way—not significant perhaps, for golf is only a game, but in a way that contributes to the enjoyment of life.

There were six other minor gods who applied for the position of first golf god before the deadline. All passed the background check. It was left to a one-question essay test to differentiate the candidates. The question was: What should be the main benefit of golf for the people who play it? The applicants had forty minutes to come up with a one-sentence answer.

Phor mulled over the question for thirty-nine minutes before quickly scribbling his answer. This was his winning response:

> *Golf should be an enjoyable and frequently victorious reflection of the player's philosophy of life.*

This may seem strange, given what you know about gods, but Phor has actually been humbled by his responsibility. Few, if any gods have considered that what they are responsible for is more important than they themselves are, but Phor has. He appreciates the unbounded joy of hitting the ball in the air for the first time. He has been in the hearts and the souls of people who made their first bogey, their first par, their first birdie.

Since 1822, Phor has observed more putts dropping into the hole to break 100 than there are grains of sand in Hawaii. He's loved every moment.

Phor is fully aware that for most players golf is only a game, no different from an afternoon of horseshoes, drinking beer on the backyard deck, or swapping stories at Arnold's Bar and Grill after a few lines of bowling. At the same time, he knows that golf provides to the knowledgeable the truest test of character, will, and skill outside of actual warfare. Phor is indulgent to the uninitiated and respectful of those who invest their hearts in our all-consuming game. To the degree you care about golf, Phor is more than willing to care about you.

### What Phor Wants

Phor wants so very little of the golfer; yet, he wants everything. He wants you to take care of the game. He knows that golf is a game, and that he is a minor god in the great scheme of things. He also knows that the devil is in the details. Take responsibility for the little things and the big things will be taken care of, was his idea.

Phor wants you to play golf, first and foremost, for fun. Do whatever it takes to enjoy the heck out of the day, forget bad shots, tee the ball in the fairway, never mind penalty strokes, just enjoy yourself. Once the game is fun Phor would like you to preserve it for others. Take care of the course; play by the rules; teach the game to others; learn how to be a steward of the game. Next, Phor would like you to use golf to improve your character. Learn to accept reality and choose the right club; acknowledge your strengths and give enough strokes; admit to your weaknesses and work to improve them; acknowledge that golf is only a game and keep it in perspective. Last, Phor would like you to use golf to improve the world. Just as you fix your ball mark and a couple more, allow others to make mistakes without judging; just as you pay a green fee, contribute to those less fortunate than you; just as you buy drinks at the end of the round for those you defeated, acknowledge the validity of those who oppose you.

Phor believes that he is not the center of the universe. He wants you to believe the same thing about yourself.

### How to Become Phor's Friend

You already are. Phor knows that anyone who has taken a club in hand and tried to hit a stationary golf ball has embarked on a journey of challenge and discovery. As long as you play the game as a reflection of who you are and don't obstruct others from doing the same, he will do all he can to eliminate the injuries and insults that drive people into dementia. Play the game as you want to and allow others to do the same, ensure the game retains its essence, and Phor will always be by your side.

### Guardian Golf God Pledge

*At your bidding I will bring to bear the full power of my office as the supreme golf god.*

*A Sampling of Current or Former Guardian Clients*

Jack Nicklaus, Graying Golden Bear
Nancy Lopez, Woman golfer icon
Michael Jordan, Basketball superstar
Gary Wiren, Golf instructor and author
Sean Connery, Member, R & A
Warren Buffett, Thrifty philanthropist

# Hesta

### Area of Responsibility

Anything that Phor doesn't get right and everything else that needs to get done

### Golf God Level

Super Major

### Biography

As you know, Hesta was the mortal sister (stepsister) of one of the ancient Greek gods, namely Eris. To understand Hesta you have to understand Eris, which is pretty easy to do. Eris was the daughter of Zeus and Hera, and was the goddess of discord. She was not a popular god and was often snubbed by other gods and mankind. Sometimes this resulted in Eris seeking revenge; in fact, it always resulted in Eris seeking revenge. For example, when she was not invited to one of the god weddings she managed to start the ball rolling toward the Trojan War.

It is safe to say that any mortal relative of Eris would quickly learn the value of avoiding discord, which Hesta was able to do quite well. When you invite the goddess of discord to a party you'd better be sure that party is well organized. Hesta was a whiz at handling details. Everyone was invited to her parties, everyone was welcome, and everyone received a thoughtful thank-you note for attending. Gods and mortals alike adored her.

Better than anyone else of her era Hesta knew that everyone who tried to accomplish anything was uncertain at times. She vowed to make it easier for everyone to relate to one another, to help one another, and more than anything else to appreciate one another.

Hesta was born in 370 B.C.E. and died in 323 B.C.E., the same year as Alexander the Great. As a relative of one of the gods, Hesta upon her death was afforded luxurious accommodations in any one of the many heavens that existed at that time. Wisely she chose Limbo, a relatively new heaven that was designed specifically for transients shopping for the best deal. Anyone in Limbo could stay in Limbo for as long as they needed to make a decision or until three thousand years had passed, whichever came first.

As a resident of Limbo Hesta had the opportunity to observe life on earth as it evolved from pantheism to monotheism. You would think that moving from many gods to only one would simplify things. Yet, even as late as the nineteenth century, Hesta was unsure of where she should go to best serve the needs of others.

Two things made up her mind. She had been observing with great interest how the role of women had been evolving. When she was alive, women were afforded almost the same rights as men. She watched as her gender became second-class throughout Europe and Asia. Sometime around 1830 she had had enough and wanted to do something about women's rights.

She became aware of the new golf god Phor at about the same time. She checked him out, liked what she saw, and decided to make something happen. A game of golf was arranged at Dornoch in the far north of Scotland.

She could have played the helpless beginner, but that wasn't Hesta's style. She took lessons for two weeks prior to their date and belted the ball with as much vigor as any man. However, she flirted shamelessly during and after the match. Phor was a puddle of glop when she suggested that she become a golf god. Her offer was impossible to turn down. "I'll do that which you choose not to do or for some reason cannot do," she said. "I'll ensure the game is one of passion and compassion." She kissed him long and hard on the lips and the match was made. Hesta became the second golf god.

### What Hesta Wants

Hesta's focus is on the companionability of golf. Just as the rules of golf state that a single on the course has no standing, Hesta believes and endorses the idea that golf is first and foremost a social game. Opponents in a match can spend four hours walking and talking with one another while trying to beat each other's brains in. In other competitions opponents are on opposite sides of the venue. In golf they can walk side by side down the fairway, as Annika Sorenstam and Pat Hurst did in the 2006 U.S. Open play-off.

Just as golf is a microcosm of life for Phor, with its agony and ecstasy, its trial by fire and ultimate personal responsibility, golf is a microcosm of humanism for Hesta, reflecting the responsibility all of us have for our fellow beings. She wants you to be aware of that element of the game, respect it, and take responsibility for it. She wants you to respect your playing companions, those ahead and behind you on the course, all those who play the game and those who someday will. It's a daunting task. But no more difficult than hitting a flop shot or sinking a downhill ten-foot putt to break ninety.

### How to Become Hesta's Friend

Hesta has little interest in how well you play golf. She is, however, interested in your character. And she has considerable power on her own and though all the other golf gods, including Phor. She has made sure that if you lose your temper on the course you are nine times more likely to lose the match than if you keep your composure.

More than any other golf god, Hesta cares about you. You can screw up a thousand times yet begin each round with a clean slate. You can be a total jerk for seventeen holes and redeem yourself on eighteen. However it's a whole lot easier if you're simply kind to other golfers all the time. Enjoy them for who they are rather than how well they play.

About one-twentieth of one percent of golfers are listed in her black book. These players have cheated others, been surly to workers, made hurtful remarks, and keep on doing it. Hesta knows that some have been taken over by the golf demons, and she has great sympathy for them. Others in her black book are mean-spirited. For those she has no mercy.

If you're not in her black book (and if you're reading these pages, you are probably not) have fun, be happy, care about yourself and others, and Hesta will treat you well and so will your fellow golfers.

### Guardian Golf God Pledge

*No one will be neglected as I watch over them. I will be there to help you when you only whisper my name. However, I am most interested in your enjoyment of the game and not so much interested in your score or your distance off the tee. Call on me for fulfillment and content-ment, far richer rewards than mere victory.*

### A Sampling of Current or Former Guardian Clients

Winston Churchill, Prime Minister
Dwight D. Eisenhower, U.S. President
Bob Jones, Amateur golfer
Darren Clarke, Professional golfer
Davis Love III, Professional golfer
Paul McGinley, Professional golfer

# The Major Golf Gods

BOK  SARAH WINSTON
BINGO  BANGO
BONGO  OOPMON
OBSISSA  MAAT

Major golf gods are major golf gods because that's what golf needs at the time. A minor golf god can grow to become a major golf god, and a major golf god can lose influence and become a minor golf god or even be forced into early retirement.

The role of a major golf god is to ensure the fulfillment of the vision that Phor and Hesta created: that "Golf will be the game loved and enjoyed by players for the next 10,000 years."

They report to Phor twice a year: on October 11 for Northern hemisphere activities and April 13 for Southern hemisphere activities. Among report items are the numbers for:

- Rounds played
- Number of players (male and female, kids and adults)
- Average cost per round
- Clubs thrown
- Rounds abandoned
- Players invited to play through
- Miles walked compared to miles driven or ridden
- Shortest putt missed (and counted)
- Lipouts (180s, 360s, and 540s)
- Trees hit (plus multiple trees hit)
- Lost balls (and found balls)
- Marriages and divorces among golfers

Phor uses these data to define the health of the game.

Major golf gods also meet together twice a year about a week prior to reporting to Phor. These meetings are almost always held in Hong Kong because so many of the golf gods love the availability of superb Peking duck adjacent to horse racing.

Otherwise, the major golf gods pretty much stick to themselves. They certainly socialize and take time off, but as major golf gods they know their primary responsibility lies with taking care of golf and golfers.

# Bok

### Area of Responsibility

The golf swing

### Golf God Level

Major

### Biography

Bok is one of the older golf gods. He was recruited by Phor when Phor realized that golf was more complicated than he thought. Bok is a second cousin to the Muse and plays tenor sax in his spare time. His favorite musician is Dave Brubeck.

Bok has aged well since he was brought on board in the mid-1800s. He had to adjust to the invention of the gutta percha ball just as he was getting started, then to the Haskell ball, steel shafts, the air game replacing the ground game, and the invention of metal woods. He also had to adapt to the growing number of female players and to formulate ways in which those with various physical impairments could enjoy the game.

Bok prides himself with accepting, even encouraging diversity in the golf swing. One of his successes was Lee Trevino. More recently he helped Jim Furyk and his looping swing to the pinnacle of the game when Furyk won the 2003 U.S. Open. Bok's intent is to let everyone know the swing can and should be individualized. He hates swing theories. At the same time, however, as a musician he is interested in rhythm and grace. If you could imagine the number and style of all the golf swings in the world, you'd have some idea of the immensity of Bok's responsibility in watching over such a multitude.

### What Bok Wants

Bok wants every golfer's swing to be as rhythmic and effective as possible. His biggest challenge is accepting that not everyone wants to practice enough to develop an elegant yet effective swing and that today's power game is to grace what a sock in the jaw is to subtlety.

### How to Become Bok's Friend

Take at least three lessons. Blame him for a bad swing in direct proportion to the practice time you put in. To get on his good side tell your playing companions that you're working on swinging smoothly rather than hard. Every time you swing so you hardly feel the club hit the ball, say, "Thanks, Bok," out loud. If you acknowledge his interest he'll help you groove a great swing.

There is one other thing you can do to get on his good side. Make sure you "finish" your backswing before you begin your swing at the ball. Pause at the top, think "Bok," and be on your way.

Bok would never do anything to harm someone's swing. He is one of the most positive and helpful of the golf gods. Swing smoothly, with rhythm, and he'll help you all he can. Swing the club like you're beating out a fire, and he'll simply look elsewhere for someone who wants his help.

### Guardian Golf God Pledge

*Ernie Els called on me—I can do the same for you as I did for him. Make me your guardian, and I will make your swing beautiful and effective.*

### A Sampling of Current or Former Guardian Clients

Fred Couples, Professional golfer
Paula Creamer, Professional golfer
Lorena Ochoa, Professional golfer
Seve Ballesteros, Professional golfer
Vijay Singh, Professional golfer
Grace Park, Professional golfer

# Sarah Winston

## Area of Responsibility

Beginning women golfers, others as time permits, and the grace of the game

## Golf God Level

Major

## Biography

Ms. Winston was created by Phor and Hesta, almost as their child when more and more females were taking up the game in the late nineteenth century. They felt that the delicate constitutions of these women and girls needed protection against the torments of the game. Ms. Winston ushered women to shorter tees, nine holes rather than eighteen, and voluminous skirts. Thus, initially she was as comforting as a fainting couch and just about as useful.

Ms. Winston thought her role was to help women avoid overexertion. She quickly learned to encourage growing numbers of women players to enjoy all aspects of golf. This meant taking on a teaching role prompting women to expand their boundaries, including taking more responsibility for stewardship of the game.

One of her most satisfying accomplishments was to finally enable a woman, Judy Bell, to become the first female to serve on the USGA's fifteen-member executive committee in 1987. In 1996–97 Bell served as USGA president, the first woman to do so in the organization's 109-year history.

Ms. Winston is an optimist. She sees great things on the horizon. Anyone who promotes women's golf will make her happy and will reap the rewards of more pleasurable golf.

## What Ms. Winston Wants

Respect for new women players from experienced players, especially men. For new women players not to make fools of themselves.

### How to Become Ms. Winston's Friend

Don't make fun of women players, especially new ones. When scorned, Ms. Winston can make life miserable. (Note to men: Appreciate that women are different, enjoy the game as much as you, deserve to have full rights and privileges, and when given a chance are enjoyable playing companions.)

New women golfers can score points with Ms. Winston in a number of ways. Join the Executive Women's Golf Association. Don't stand at address then suddenly bend your knees. Take lessons so you can avoid the common chopping motion, and learn how to hit the ball with vigor. She'll love you and make sure your day on the course is an enjoyable one. Women tour professionals should learn to align themselves without the aid of a caddie.

You will know you have offended Ms. Winston if two or more of your tee shots fail to advance more than five yards in front of the forward tees; if you find a pink ball while looking for your white one; or if you say to any of your playing partners something like "nice shot, Alice" or "did you hit that one with your purse?"

You can repent by doing one or more of the following: Tip the cart girl ten dollars, invite a group of women golfers to play through, go shopping with the wife, take a lesson from a woman pro, or vacuum the living room without being asked.

### Guardian Golf God Pledge

*I would like all new female players (and those transgendered ladies) to count on me. I will provide you with knowledge and grace, and, if you wish, a kickass swing like Annika Sorenstam's.*

### A Sampling of Current or Former Guardian Clients

Margaret Thatcher, Prime Minister
Sandra Bullock, Actress
Martha Burk, Level playing field activist
Martha Stewart, Homemaker, businesswoman
Christine Gregoire, Governor (Washington state)
Christine de Noir, Exotic dancer

# *Bingo*

*Area of Responsibility*

The grip

*Golf God Level*

Major

*Biography*

The phrase "get a grip" refers to a situation in which someone is losing control. Among the golf gods the phrase represents one of the famous ways they influenced the world beyond the game of golf. Golf god Bingo made up the phrase when she was looking for a quick way to remind golfers to pay attention to how they held the club. When she noticed a bad grip she would whisper in the person's ear at the golf god frequency to "get a grip." This message was extremely high pitched with an equally extreme low amplitude (something only golf gods can do). The experience of this communication is midway between a dream and a hallucination. Many golfers do improve their grips after hearing this message a number of times, some by purchasing new ones, others by getting a lesson in how to correctly hold the club.

Inspiring people to tell each other to get a grip, however, was not Bingo's intent when she made the phrase up. It seems that a number of teenage golfers she whispered to in California began using this phrase themselves, usually mumbled in a sullen tone to their parents.

Bingo's job was to help golfers become comfortable with the second most unnatural grip in sports. Hesta initially noticed the importance of the grip when English professional Harry Vardon popularized a grip that had first been used twenty years earlier. Vardon did more than just introduce the grip during his trip to the United States in 1900. He caught Hesta's interest with his beautiful upright swing, which stood in significant contrast to the more usual flat, almost chopping or swaying motion used at the time.

On her own, Hesta sought a golf god of the grip during the 1950s. She found one in northern India in a small village south-west of Darjeeling, just in time to guide the greatest golfer of the twentieth century. The village had recently completed a construction project, so everyone had access to running water. The old god of the well was no longer needed and really hadn't been for at least two generations. She was slowly dying. Hesta asked her to become the new golf god of golf grips, and she read-ily accepted.

Her first job, begun immediately, was to whisper in the ear of a fellow named Jack Nicklaus. He was thinking of trying the Vardon grip, the one all his friends and most players on the pro-fessional tours used. As a child he started out with a baseball grip, as most kids do then switched to an interlocking grip in

*Bingo*

which the first finger of the left hand interlocks with the little finger of the right hand. It's a lady's grip. She whispered in Jack's ear every night, "keep your grip, keep your grip." And from then on he has kept the interlocking golf grip and for the most part kept his grip everywhere else too.

## What Bingo Wants

She wants you to realize that the grip is the most important part of the golf swing. How many players (especially lefties) have you seen who hold their top hand turned so far over the club (clockwise as a right-hander looks down) that their arms are twisted, with the bottom hand almost under the club? The only swing available with such a setup is a huge sway for a backswing and an equally huge lunge back at the ball. She wants most players to use a neutral grip. She wants the "Vs" formed by the thumb and first finger on each hand to be parallel. She wants people with small or weak hands to use the interlocking grip, just like Jack.

Most of all she wants people to understand that the grip is the player's only connection to the ball and that the grip has to allow free movement of the hands through the impact area. Any tension in the grip inhibits the freewheeling action that is necessary to a good swing. She wants all golfers to know that nothing in golf is more important than the grip.

Hold your club with the same affection and gentle strength that you would hold Bingo's hand. She is a major golf god, as befits the importance of the grip.

## How to Become Bingo's Friend

If you get a golf lesson, make sure you include an evaluation of your grip. Be like her star pupil Jack, and reassess your grip at least once a year. Think about and examine how your grip may influence your swing. Make sure your "Vs" point where they should. Although her individual power is limited, Bingo is admired by many other golf gods, and they all want to do her favors.

Here's the catch. Now that you've read about the importance of the grip and that Bingo is a major golf god with major golf god power, failure to improve your grip if it is faulty, or failure to evaluate your grip periodically if it is sound, will begin your sad but steady decent into golf purgatory as the golf gods chop your game into bite-sized veal cutlets, one triple bogey at a time.

### Guardian Golf God Pledge

*I promise that I will give you the grip of a fourteen-year-old girl, creating the most perfect blend of grace and strength for a good golf swing, no matter how tense you may be, how tight the match is, or how hard your swing.*

### A Sampling of Current or Former Guardian Clients

Chris DiMarco, Professional golfer
Sergio Garcia, Professional golfer
Mike Weir, Professional golfer
Cristie Kerr, Professional golfer
Hee-Won Han, Professional golfer
Sophie Gustafson, Professional golfer

# Bango

*Area of Responsibility*

The release

*Golf God Level*

Major

*Biography*

Bango is Bingo's brother, brought along by Hesta in the middle 1950s when she recruited Bingo. Bango was the extremely minor god of frogs in the well water, or more specifically the absence of frogs in the well, near the village where Bingo was the god of the well itself. When given the chance of becoming the golf god of the release, he jumped on it.

By default he is also the golf god of the wrist-cock, for without a wrist-cock there is not much chance of a release. Unfortunately, Bango suffers from a form of dyskinesia. He has a hard time comprehending and discerning right and left, and also any movement from side to side, front to back, or back to front. When he telepathically communicates with a golfer he should be able to describe a right-hander's release simply as "right hand over the left," but he can't. He ends up with something like "the right hand turns round along with the left as both slide forward toward the ball but the left has to lead until it suddenly twists out of the way with the butt of the left hand falling toward the ground followed by the butt part of the right hand but with the butt of the right hand quickly being lifted as the top of the right hand regains the top position after impact."

Even more unfortunately, Bango has made it a quest to communicate his ever changing description of the wrist-cock and release to every golfer at least twice a year. The effect of his dedication can be seen on the first tee of most any course. Women, who are most likely to try to follow his subliminal instructions, can be seen lifting the club almost vertically, pointing it straight in the air without a wrist-cock, then pushing with the right hand through the ball with no discernible release—pretty much

*Bango*

exactly what Bango inadvertently told them to do. Perhaps half of male golfers also avoid a real wrist-cock and don't benefit much from the release but get distance by throwing body mass behind the swing.

### What Bango Wants

He is most interested in two things: golfers who know nothing about the release keeping their swing advice to themselves, and for all golfers to be aware of his flapjack drill. In this drill, with both arms pointing right, right-handed golfers place both hands together palm to palm with the left hand on top of the right hand. The arms then rotate in front of the body with the hands slowly flipping over. The timing is such that the hands are vertical when the arms are directly in front of the body, and the right hand is on top when the arms are fully over to the left. When this flip can be accomplished comfortably the golfer practices the same motion but with the hands placed in the position of a golf grip.

## How to Become Bango's Friend

Tell every golfer you know that you think the wrist-cock and the release are the most important ingredients of a good golf swing. If you see players who swing with no wrist-cock or release, teach them Bango's little flapjack drill. If after reading his description and interests you don't have a good release and don't make the effort to learn how, Bango is fully capable of causing you to suffer a severe case of carpal tunnel syndrome just as you exit your car at the Lodge at Pebble Beach for a glorious weeklong golf vacation.

## Guardian Golf God Pledge

*When I am your guardian golf god, I will provide you with an extra twenty-miles-per-hour clubhead speed with every club. And, if chosen three times in a row, I will enable you to hit fades and draws at will just by wanting to.*

## A Sampling of Current or Former Guardian Clients

Moe Norman, Professional golfer
Ryan Palmer, Professional golfer
Juli Inkster, Professional golfer
Dottie Pepper, Professional golfer and commentator
Jeff Daniels, Actor
Michael Eskew, Businessman

# Bongo

*Area of Responsibility*

Balance

*Golf God Level*

Major

*Biography*

Bongo is the sister of both Bingo and Bango. She was the god of people falling into the well. None did for the 300 years it was used, so she was regarded as a warm and benevolent god. When asked to accompany her siblings she also agreed quickly and suggested that she become the golf god of balance.

To make sure she understood the dynamics of golf she studied the human activities that produce power with balance, something of which she was sure Hesta would approve. She looked at ballet, the Olympic throwing events, long jumping, pole vaulting, the 100- and 200-meter dashes, volleyball spiking, fastball pitchers (both hardball and softball), card dealing, scull rowing, and weight lifting's clean and jerk.

She also studied the mechanics of the golf swing. Here she learned the importance of the hips in producing power and how the arms actually slow at impact, which enables her brother's release motion to occur.

Unlike her brother and sister, Bongo doesn't try to tell golfers anything. She believes that anyone who swings with balance will be justly rewarded and anyone who doesn't will suffer appropriately, except for kids and the mentally challenged. She encourages these two groups to swing with abandon by making it fun and allowing for the occasional great hit, high and far.

*What Bongo Wants*

More than anything Bongo wants golfers to understand that balance is the most important element of the golf swing. Violent Neanderthal slashes at the ball make her cringe. She loves the grace of Fred Couples (and has had a crush on him since he was nineteen). She hopes for a slow, steady, and gentle transition from the backswing into the downswing so every player achieves the elusive sequence of hitting the ball from the ground up. She wants all golfers to play the game between their feet.

### How to Become Bongo's Friend

This is critical. Bongo doesn't go in for punishing errant golfers, ones who swipe and slash at the ball. It doesn't bother her if a golfer reverses weight, falls backward, or falls forward. Balance, she believes, is its own reward. However, Hesta cares. Hesta cares a lot about Bongo, Bango, and Bingo. Hesta cares a

*Bongo*

lot about what they preach. You have to appease Hesta in this area more than anything. This advice may sound strange, but it's the best way. On the first tee, do a little dance. Swing your hips side to side and with your hands close together in front of you stick out your elbows and move them up and down. Do this and sing, "I'm a gonna Bingo, Bango, and Bongo today. Yeah, yeah." You may feel ridiculous for a moment but if you can win favor you'll swing better than ever and hit better than ever, score better than ever, enjoy the game better than ever, and be more popular and adored everywhere.

You get a substantial reward for just a little dance. Go for it.

### Guardian Golf God Pledge

*I would be honored to be chosen as your guardian golf god. If so chosen, I promise that I will ensure your swing will become as balanced as Fred Couples's swing and almost as effective. All I ask is that you try to swing within yourself. That will make both of us happy.*

### A Sampling of Current or Former Guardian Clients

Gary Player, Professional golfer
Casey Martin, Professional golfer, role model
Mikhail Baryshnikov, Dancer
Evel Knievel Jr., Daredevil
Tip O'Neill, Politician
Lance Armstrong, Bicyclist

# Oopmon

*Area of Responsibility*

Putting

*Golf God Level*

Major (used to be Minor)

*Biography*

Originally Oopmon was the only god of Poolifusas, a small island in the South Pacific about 800 miles east of Fiji. He was worshipped in elaborate ceremonies twice a week, and a virgin was sacrificed for him once a year. Goddom was good for Oopmon for about 1,000 years. Then the missionaries came, bringing with them modern ideas and half a dozen diseases. All the islanders died within a generation, and the missionaries had to go elsewhere to save the natives.

Left on his own Oopmon slowly went crazy, staying alive only because he had been a major god for so long. He spent his mornings drawing miles of long parallel lines in the sand with a stick and his afternoons smoothing out the lines with his hands. Evenings were spent digging small holes. During the long nights he located the holes with his bare feet and filled them again by pushing sand in with his toes.

Just prior to going totally insane Oopmon heard the call for golf gods, applied, and was chosen to become the god of putting when Phor realized that he would go raving mad if he didn't quickly have something useful to do.

Once he was made the golf god of putting, Oopmon put his own spin on this part of the game. In the olden days putting was not much more than a hopeful chip from near the hole. "Greens" were no different from fairways. A miss from three feet could be shrugged off as bad luck, rub of the green, or an unfortunate deflection from a bump in the turf. Oopmon decided that not enough was asked for as the player got nearer the final objective. He wanted ultra-smooth greens so there would be no one to blame but the golfer when the ball failed to drop in the hole.

Naturally, he set up shop in the United States, the land of "more is better," and ultimately settled in Augusta, Georgia. In the human form of a greenskeeper he spent his days mowing and rolling Augusta National's splendid greens. When he started, and contrary to what you may have heard, Augusta greens were as rough and long as any municipal would keep them. As for the immensely wealthy and hoary members of the club there was no reason for anyone to want anything else: they didn't want to spend any more money than they needed to, they wouldn't notice any difference, and they couldn't putt worth a lick anyway. Using this lack of awareness to his advantage, Oopmon began an insidious process that took over twenty-two years from start to finish. He cut the grass shorter and shorter by countless 1/248-inch steps at a time. It was like boiling a frog so slowly from cool water to hot that the frog never notices a thing. The members never suspected that their greens were slowly but surely becoming like slabs of marble.

Diabolically, he also began rolling the greens so smooth that only members could putt successfully on them. Guests could never learn to hit the putts softly enough to stay on the green.

Since most Augusta National members are members of other clubs, this extremely short grass and rolled greens approach was transferred to other clubs, most of them among the best in the world.

Many want-to-be clubs tried the same thing. Today you can see Oopmon's impact at almost every country club and daily-fee course where the powers that be shave the greens within a fraction of their lives. Even the USGA, supposedly the protector of the game, is attempting to invent grasses that can withstand being mutilated for the sake of speed.

### What Oopmon Wants

Unlike every other golf god, what Oopmon wants is not related to the enjoyment of golf by the golfer. Oopmon wants only to see greens become like glass. His objective is for every putt to run exactly true to how it was struck, never to waver off line, and to run on as if powered from within. He loves straight lines. He knows that faster greens means flatter greens. His ideal is a green that is totally flat, made of glass, where every putt runs straight.

### How to Become Oopmon's Friend

You can't. Oopmon doesn't care about you. He rarely listens. He rarely responds. He is in love with greens, not golfers. The first thing you can do if you want golf god help with your putting is to appeal to a golf god who has helped you in the past, or to another golf god you might be able to do favors for. The way the golf gods are currently set up, sorry to say, you're pretty much on your own on the green. Unless—unless you are one of the few who truly understand that every putt is a straight putt. You, he will help.

### Guardian Golf God Pledge

*Use me as your guardian golf god if you want to or don't. It's up to you. Do whatever you want. I'm really busy.*

### A Sampling of Current or Former Guardian Clients

Loren Roberts, Professional golfer
Scott Verplank, Professional golfer
Bernhard Langer, Professional golfer
Morris Hatalsky, Professional golfer
Bill Brown, Amateur golfer
Clifford Roberts, Fearsome chairman

# *Obsissa*

### *Area of Responsibility*

Distance

### *Golf God Level*

Major (used to be Minor)

### *Biography*

Unfortunately, as some think anyway, Obsissa is quickly becoming a powerful major golf god. Distance as seen in the length of courses, in the length of tee shots, in the length a putt will travel (increased green speed equals increased distance), the length of time to play a round, even in the length of greens (size is everything), is taking over golf. Why? To the curse of us all, Obsissa, the golf god of distance, is a teenager.

Although this is not widely known, some gods stay the same age and others grow older. Actually, they all grow older but some at rates much slower than others. And, of course, a god becomes a god at a specific age and gets older from there. But then, this doesn't always happen either. Some gods are made younger after asking for it, or when it just seems the right thing to do. Phor, for example, was a god for a long time before becoming a golf god. He was older than many of the other golf gods when he became a golf god and is aging more slowly than most other golf gods, currently at the rate of about one year for every 678 earth circles around the sun. It is not known exactly when Obsissa was born. No one is saying, but he was born in either the late 1920s or the early 1930s.

Obsissa was the illegitimate son of Susan by an unknown father who could have been a golf god. Susan was a golf god at time of conception, so her son automatically became a golf god too when he turned fifteen in earth years—if, of course, he wanted to become one, which he did. And he wanted to stay fifteen, which he has.

Like most golf gods Obsissa could transform himself in any number of ways. On occasion golf gods jump into the thoughts and feelings of mortals. A favorite for Obsissa was being inside Elvis Presley in the 1950s and so was being inside President Nixon during his last two years in office. Obsissa would jump into their skins and take over their minds for weeks on end. He thought it was a hoot. This is understandable, given that Obsissa has the mental age of a fifteen year old, and his main purpose in life is to cause havoc.

His mother Susan would try to control him, but it was a nearly impossible job. He'd disappear for a month or two, and it was only by carefully studying the behavior of famous people that she could discover where he was and whom he had taken over.

He really messed up some people, such as baseball player Bill Buckner. Obsissa defends himself when someone brings up Buckner's misplay of a slow roller down the first base line during a play-off, saying, "Hey, I was distracted, give me a break." His mother thinks there are many victims of his interference, including two recent U.S. presidents, George W. Bush and earlier Bill Clinton; one somewhat nutty popular evangelist; a governor of California; a Tour de France winner (and blame was placed on drugs); actor Tom Cruise; the executive leadership of Enron; and, she fears, her favorite actor, Hugh Grant.

As far as golf is concerned Obsissa has only one interest: the ball must be hit so hard and so far that distance becomes the only part of golf that matters. When any big hitter on the tour really launches one, Obsissa is in the player and in everyone who yells, "You da man!" Obsissa's response to these blasts is frighteningly similar to the reaction a pyromaniac has watching a building burn down.

Obsissa gloms onto anyone who is beginning to make a decision about hitting a driver or laying up with an iron. He is there when the owner of the new course is discussing hole length with the architect. He is there when the greens committee is discussing tournament conditions. Obsissa exemplifies the quintessential American belief that "If some is good, a lot more is better."

With the energy of youth Obsissa tries to make everyone do what he wants. If you hit a beautiful drive just about as far as you can, and on the next tee you even fleetingly think about trying for five more yards, Obsissa is saying "go for it" and will help you swing out of your socks.

## What Obsissa Wants

He is not much interested in hitting irons a long way although he encourages people to try to hit them farther than is reasonable. His overriding focus is distance with a driver off the tee or off the turf. A secondary interest is effort. It pleases him when a person slashes extremely hard at the ball, especially when there is no regard for accuracy (this may be a bit of adolescent rebellion) or physical well-being. Obsissa is turned on by distance. If you hit your driver a hundred yards, he wants you to try for a hundred and fifty. If you can hit it three hundred yards, he asks why not go for four hundred. If the green is reachable from the tee by a King Kong blast, you should try it no matter how the match stands.

## How to Become Obsissa's Friend

Go for the bomb from every tee. Less than that, you're a wuss. Often enough he'll help you out. You've already experienced the primal pleasure of taking it deep, so there is no reason not to go for it every time you feel like it. Phil Mickelson had Obsissa for his guardian golf god for six years in a row. See how it worked for him?

## Guardian Golf God Pledge

*Okay, this is the deal. Golf is a power game, no question. You buy the biggest mother of a driver you can find, and I'll make sure you mash your tee ball beyond everybody else. And just in case another guy has asked me, you swing harder, I make it go farther, no questions asked.*

## A Sampling of Current or Former Guardian Clients

Laurie Davies, Professional golfer
John Daly, Professional golfer
J. J. Henry, Professional golfer
Tom Kite, Professional golfer
Corey Pavin, Professional golfer
Gerry James, Long drive champion

# *Maat*

### *Area of Responsibility*

Nineteenth hole

### *Golf God Level*

Major

### *Biography*

As the great-grandnephew of Bacchus, Maat has been around for a long time and has been a sober alcoholic for about three hundred years. He had a great situation. As a close relative of a god he was immortal, but as a nongod, he had none of the responsibilities. His life was like that of maybe a George Hamilton or a Paris Hilton, only better. He was invited to all the parties, was a charming guest, got drunk, and went home. This went on for hundreds of years.

Somewhere in the seventeenth century he sensed that something was missing. He decided no more wine, no more beer, no more mead, no more nothing. It took about forty years to get his blood alcohol level below 4.8, but eventually he could think clearly, he could sleep through the night, and, most importantly, he could remember what happened the day before. Life became interesting again.

After a round of golf at the Crail links in Scotland in 1877, Maat was sitting with Phor, Hesta, and a few other gods and spirit people. He was drinking his usual Arnold Palmer. (But of course, they didn't call it an Arnold Palmer in those days. It was called "that drink with equal portions of lemonade and cold tea.") The company was grand and the conversation animated. They were all having a great time. Hesta was the first to say it: "This should always be part of a golfing day." Phor agreed, saying, "Golf should have a nineteenth hole and this should be it." Everyone at the table thought this was a good idea.

Hesta looked at Phor. "Why don't you make it so?" Phor looked around, saw Maat, and said, "Maat, how about becoming a golf god? About time you took a position. How about becoming the golf god of the nineteenth hole?" And thus it was so.

### What Maat Wants

The nineteenth hole is a multipurpose decompression chamber. For quite a few golfers it is the time and place to discharge severe emotional overload. To miss this time for discharge is to chance rage on the road, kicks at the dog, yells at the spouse, and a generally sour end to the day.

For a smaller yet still significant number of golfers the nineteenth hole is a platform from which to relive glorious moments on the links, when the sun was shining, the birds were singing, and the player hit shots exactly as planned.

On a more practical level it is the time to do accounting, both on the scorecard and in the exchange of cash. The nineteenth hole is the coda to the eighteen stories that came before.

*Maat*

Without a nineteenth hole golf would be like a story without an end, sex without the "Oh," a job without a paycheck.

Maat wants you to take this part of golf seriously. Do not finish your game and rush elsewhere. The game doesn't end until there are no more drinks or no more stories or no more need for emotional repair. The nineteenth hole isn't over until every player confirms that golf is the best game in the world and no one present is thinking of giving it up.

### How to Be Maat's Friend

If you have had an especially good day, do not tell success stories in any greater ratio to the horror stories of your playing companions than 3:5. That's right; you tell of your glories less than you allow others to share their pain.

On the other hand, if you have suffered the torments of the damned, for the most part you have deserved them, for the golf gods have done to you what they thought you deserved. At least this is true for some of you. Others have only been victims of the inherent nature of the game, or have been innocent recipients of accidents of the golf gods, and should be offered great amounts of sympathy. If you must share your stories of despair, share no more than three.

If for any reason you feel the need to break these guidelines you can avoid Maat's wrath by this simple expedient: for every glory story over the limit, pay your playing companions two dollars each. If you must describe your great front nine in its entirety, that'll cost you ten bucks each. For describing your wondrous back nine, that is only eight dollars because often stories of the conclusion of the match are more interesting.

Horror stories are the same but will cost you less for each hole, only fifty cents, but more for each nine: fifteen dollars for the front, twenty dollars for the back (nobody likes a poor loser).

Winners, of course, buy the first round and sometimes the second if the victory was a large one. The idea is that everyone leaves the nineteenth hole an equal, glory stories and gory stories all told, smiles and handshakes exchanged, and the next game scheduled.

## Guardian Golf God Pledge

*I'd love being your guardian golf god. If I am, you will be able to describe your game in infinite detail for as long as you like without cost, and your playing companions and anyone else within earshot will hang on every word and ask for more. In addition, if you're playing in a tournament and begin composing your victory speech before you have actually won, I will do my best to help that speech become a reality in spite of your not playing one shot at a time like you're supposed to. (For the latter benefit, you must give away golf balls to as many kid spectators as you can after you realize the huge mental error you just made.)*

## A Sampling of Current or Former Guardian Clients

Fuzzy Zoeller, Professional golfer
Christy O'Connor Jr., Professional golfer
Ian Woosnam, Professional golfer
Peter Jacobsen, Professional golfer
Bette Midler, Diva
Danny Williams, Amateur golfer

# The Major-Minor
# Golf Gods

MASFEL      OTOM
WHINSOMCH      SUSAN
NOGOEH

These golf gods are in transition, gaining or losing power and increasing or decreasing in influence. If the major golf gods can be viewed as the starters on a major-league baseball team, the major-minor golf gods are like the bench warmers; some will become starters and some will be sent down to the minor leagues. A few will remain major-minor gods for a long time. It all depends on the direction golf takes.

Claak, for example, was the major-minor golf god of golf spikes until his retirement. Once he observed that steel spikes were going the way of buggy whips he turned in his badge and headed for greener pastures. He began as a minor god, advanced to major status during the 1950s, 1960s, and 1970s, then swiftly declined to a minor golf god and is now a gone golf god.

Of all the golf gods the major-minor golf gods are the most intense. It is hard being between the two golf god levels, never sure if you're going up or down. As a result, sometimes they try too hard and mess things up. Sometimes they get a little depressed and let things go. They can get cranky, moody, and irritated with each other. Investing in a major-minor golf god is a bit like investing in the stock market: you can go up, you can go down, you can even stay the same, but usually you're on a ride somewhere—and you're not in control.

The major-minor golf gods care a lot, may get carried away sometimes, but will give you great effort when called upon.

# Masfel

## *Area of Responsibility*

Self-awareness

## *Golf God Level*

Major-Minor (formerly a Major golf god—but things can change quickly, and Masfel may already have dropped to Minor status)

## *Biography*

In his original form Masfel was a four-pound rock. He was situated off to the east side of a small waterfall in an area that is now northeast Sydney, Australia. Unlike most other rocks, which are totally without intelligence, Masfel was a bright, insightful, and observant rock. He didn't sit on the side of that stream oblivious of the world around him like his rock friends. No, sir. He wondered about things. While the continents were drifting apart he was calculating velocities and vectors. He knew 500,000 years before it happened that Australia would end up where it did.

But for all his intelligence and hard thinking, after six billion years of being a rock, Masfel got bored. He would have stayed bored, too, except for a phenomenal bit of luck. During the early years of British colonialism there were hundreds upon hundreds of young English gentlemen crawling all over the place exploring one thing after another. Most, of course, wouldn't know an artifact from an Aborigine but they each had to take back to Mother England all sorts of precious treasures. Luckily, one such intrepid explorer picked up Masfel, put him in a sack, and took him back to London.

There he stayed up high on a shelf for about 150 years until the newly hired maid tossed him over the back fence. Over the fence was a golf course. On that golf course Phor was checking out how his game was developing. When he walked courses Phor took human form, sometimes as a milkmaid out for a walk, sometimes as a boy truant from school, and sometimes as a stooped old man, barely able to take one more step. This day he was the boy hopping, skipping, and generally having a good time until he stepped on the side of Masfel and twisted his ankle. Down he went cursing like a Boson's Mate. "Sorry," Masfel said. "I didn't see you coming. I should have jumped out of the way." Phor immediately started laughing, and the two, rock and golf god, began an earnest conversation about rocks and dirt and rivers and all sorts of things. At some point Masfel brought up being bored. By this time Phor was greatly impressed by the intelligence of the rock and offered this suggestion: "Would you like to become a golf god? I can make you one, and I think it would be just perfect for you." Masfel said he would like that. "I can be quite steady and even tempered, and I know myself so very well. Perhaps I can be the golf god of self-awareness." And Phor agreed.

*Masfel*

## What Masfel Wants

Most golfers have no idea Masfel exists. Golfers just play golf the same way they approach everything else. For the longest time, for example, the PGA Tour's Phil Mickelson was totally oblivious as to how his gambling style would never work in major tournaments. This obliviousness is the norm at all levels of play. Usually wives are needed to help the male golfer develop even the smallest degree of self-awareness. It's as if men are like overexcited puppies ceaselessly banging against the sliding glass door to get to the food dish on the other side. Rare is the man who declares, "This isn't working; maybe I need to change what I'm doing." To men, if something isn't working, you simply do more of what you did before or get a hammer to fix it.

Women, on the other hand, are equally unaware, but it doesn't look like it since they keep asking questions about themselves. The trouble on the distaff side is that women never know the answers to their questions on their own but have to ask the nearest hapless male. (Especially the infamous and diabolical "Does this make me look fat?")

What Masfel wants, so very simply, is for the golfer to look over the situation and ask the uncomplicated question, "What's the best shot to play given the circumstances?" What he would be very happy to see is the golfer going that next step and every once in a while pondering the question, "Just what exactly is my relationship with golf?"

He hates golfers who are addicted to the game, the ones who play five or six times a week, who for all appearances play without joy. He hates people who are compulsive about keeping score, forgetting they are playing a game, outdoors, with friends.

He would love golfers to accept whatever their handicaps are, neither being proud of a low one nor despairing of a high one. He likes it when a golfer knows how far each club goes, really. He likes it when a golfer admits to weaknesses and likes it a lot when the golfer tries to improve weaknesses.

## How to Become Masfel's Friend

Be serious about the game but not critical. Try your absolute best most of the time. Play the shot that should be played, not just the shot that you want to play. Accept it when things don't go your way. If someone plays better than you and wins, congratulate the other player. If you play better and lose anyway, congratulate the other player. If you win a hard-fought match, congratulate the other player. If you lose a hard-fought match, congratulate the other player. Basically, honor your opponent, partly because without an opponent, you ain't got a game.

Honor golf as a microcosm of life. Play golf with the same values you express in your daily living. Give your opponent the benefit of the doubt just as you would your friends. Recognize, once and for all, that your view of the world is unique, and that at this moment, there are 6,496,551,862 different and equally valid points of view.

### Guardian Golf God Pledge

*If I am your golf god guardian, I pledge that you will be able to understand the second half of* Golf in the Kingdom, *be your own sports psychologist, never overestimate how far you can hit the ball, feel comfortable playing the forward tees when everyone else is hitting from further back, and end every round of golf with a new appreciation of how wonderful your life is.*

### A Sampling of Current or Former Guardian Clients

David Duval, Professional golfer
Joyce Brothers, Psychologist
Angus McIrons, Keepers of the Game
Deepak Chopra, Guru
Richard Coop, Sports psychologist
Stephen Cohen, Shivas Irons Society

# Whinsomch

## Area of Responsibility

Professional golf

## Golf God Level

Major-Minor (may become a Major very soon if not one already)

## Biography

Although golf gods are immortal, they are prone to the same types of errors and omissions as us ordinary people. In Whinsomch's case a misjudgment and just plain dumb luck brought him into being.

Somewhere in the 1880s Phor became aware of the growing interest in professional golf. Until then golf professionals were either club carriers for the wealthy players or the few odd farmers and grounds keepers who kept the green to the current standard. Phor admired the class of workmen who toiled on the links and those few who hoped to play themselves to a better life. However, he wasn't interested enough to do anything about this group himself. So he asked Hesta to find someone to become a new golf god of professional golf. Phor wanted this new god to establish standards of comportment, rewarding those who honored the game and messing with those who didn't.

Hesta, though, had no interest in professional golf or professional golfers either. She had enough to do as a golf god in her own areas, plus she had been volunteering at a pensioners' home where old people, common folk, just your regular "did-the-best-they-could-in-life" kind of people lived out their days and eventually died. She thought, why don't I make the next one to die at the old folks' home the god of professional golf?

That's what she did. She arranged to make it happen while there one day and left soon after for her hair appointment.

Unfortunately, Beverly Butler and her two-year old son Chester were visiting Grandpa Nelson the next evening when a tragic accident took place. Chester, a little scamp of a two-year old, managed to crawl under Grandpa Nelson's bed and begin chewing on the light cord. Quick as the crackle of loose electricity, Chester became a golf god.

Like those of all instant golf gods, Chester's IQ soared into very high multiple digits. However, his personality, his attitude on life, stayed where it was, smack in the middle of the terrible twos.

He had no direction at first except to do things to see what would happen. Basically he simply played havoc with the weather during professional tournaments. He loved to make flags whip on their flagstaffs. Later he would fool with the ball, giggling every time he was able to get a ball to roll right over the hole and not drop in. Players falling down in sloppy conditions were another favorite.

By the early twentieth century he was getting the hang of his job. Phor reminded him that he was to monitor the professional game, enable it to develop, but ensure that professionals did not become self-serving, selfish, swell-headed money-grubbers who thought that they were bigger than the game itself.

Walter Hagen bothered Whinsomch a bit— that stuff about sitting in a Rolls Royce and eating a catered lunch between rounds, but he still saw the point. Professionals were becoming something other than caddies who while temporarily sober played the game at a high level. Instead, he noticed that professionals related to the public, the public related to professionals, and both cared about the values of golf and both seemed to be doing okay. So for a number of years Whinsomch ignored golf and left professional golf alone. He had better things to do. He had discovered matches and cigarette lighters.

On occasion he would look over the professional game and become instantly bored as he saw the players drive from tournament to tournament in groups of two or three, often pulling a small trailer, sitting up swapping stories and drinking beers late into the night and practicing wherever they could. He noticed that the players in those days would play over asphalt if that was where the competition was.

Yet even this self-centered golf god began to observe subtle changes in the professional game. Prize money was no longer barely enough to get through a season but sufficient to buy

*Whinsomch*

ranches in Texas. Players began to fly rather than drive. Extra money no longer came from a club job but from endorsements, quite a few highly lucrative endorsements. But for the most part Whinsomch still didn't care much.

Things changed when Whinsomch heard complaining about things being unfair. Until then players had just shrugged their shoulders and said, "Course plays the same for everyone," and let it go at that. Now players were complaining of unfair conditions. This got Whinsomch's attention: nobody shall whine but he.

In spite of being the emotional equivalent of age two, Whinsomch didn't take the easy route to handle this situation by acting out. He actually thought about it and decided that one-tenth of professional golfers would henceforth remain petulant emotional two year olds, and that no matter how great their accomplishments, no matter how big their houses or how decked out in glittering bracelets their spouses, they would forever miss the point.

Whinsomch is very proud of this mature and proportional decision and is gratified most days at how well it's working.

### What Whinsomch Wants

Actually, not much. Being two years old he doesn't want to hear a bunch of moaning and groaning, especially from so-called adults. That's about it. Of course, it wouldn't hurt to say nice things every once in a while about how wonderful professional golf is. Whinsomch eats up praise, true or otherwise.

### How to Become Whinsomch's Friend

If you're a professional or intend to become one, there isn't a whole lot you have to worry about. If you allow Whinsomch to feel like he is the big guy and don't whine very much, you should be okay. Take a moment to look around you, and take comfort in the number of players who have no clue. They'll be the ones who lose out, not you. You have perspective on what life is really about. You know what to expect from golf and accept it like the adult you are. Those others don't. Ha, ha, on them. Whinsomch will become their best friend.

Keep in mind that becoming Whinsomch's friend doesn't give you that much. Once in a while he may use his power for some good, but his attention span is short enough that he often doesn't think through the consequences of his decisions. But if you want to be a professional golfer and may not have the talent or work ethic, contacting Whinsomch may be your best bet.

### Guardian Golf God Pledge

*If you're nice to me I will be nice to you. When I want to I can do about anything. We can have a lot of fun together if I'm your guardian golf god.*

### A Sampling of Current or Former Guardian Clients

This list is confidential and unavailable at this time.

# Susan

*Area of Responsibility*

Accuracy

*Golf God Level*

Major-Minor (used to be Major; may regain that status)

*Biography*

The story of Susan is being told for the first time within these pages. Phor has become enlightened about having feelings and being open and honest, and he decided to let everyone, including Hesta, learn about the origin of Susan, the golf god of accuracy.

In the olden days distance was far less important than accuracy, and that's how the game was played. Players were distinguished by how well they could play the bounces, how much control they had over distance and trajectory, how they could curve the ball in flight, and whether they could chip and putt with deadly skill.

As equipment evolved and the distances the ball traveled increased, the need for accuracy seemed as though it would become even more important. Greater distance meant that even small degrees off line resulted in greater misses. This became obvious to everyone in the early 1920s. Phor was quite sure he needed a golf god of accuracy. Normally, this would not have presented a problem. He'd just take a look at the list of names waiting in heaven to become a golf god, poll other gods about who might want the position, or just cock his ear to what was going on in the universe, and someone would rise above the crowd. And that person would become a new golf god. But his attention was elsewhere.

In the 1920s Phor was smitten by a cockney dancehall girl named Susan who hoisted her skirt, displayed her legs, and pointed her toes to his dazzled consternation. He mooned over her day and night. He transformed himself into his favorite

*Susan*

human form and haunted the dancehall every evening for weeks at a time.

Tragically, one night while performing her famous can-can with two other dancers, Susan caught the heel of her shoe on a loose board and fell nine feet into the orchestra pit. Although still alive when taken back to her squalid room, she lingered only a few days and died.

Phor was heartsick. There was nothing he loved better than watching his adored Susan turn her back to the audience, bend at the waist, and thrust her bottom to the hinterlands. He needed more of her. He must have more of her. But she was dead.

Thinking quickly, before Susan had much of a chance to contemplate the options of being dead, he offered her a proposition. He asked her to become a golf god.

"But what would I do poo-poo-pe-do?" she asked, her rosy red lips driving him crazy.

"I don't know," he admitted. "Just work with me on this so we can be together."

Susan's eyes narrowed. "Is this some sort of scam?" she asked. "Are you married?"

"I'm in a relationship. But you ... you ..."

"Don't you ... you me, buster. What's your game here?"

Phor admitted his game. Become a golf god. Live forever if you want. Retire with full benefits. Obligations are two meetings a month, monitor golf accuracy issues, ruin a golfer's life on occasion, obey Phor's every command. The usual stuff.

"Okay," she said with a curtsey, her knees bending in unison and her dimples being ever so cute. And from then on accuracy in golf became a golf god issue, sort of. But if you take a look at golf these days it really isn't much of an issue. In putting, distance is much more a factor in making putts than accuracy. In regard to approach shots to the green, greens are getting larger and larger, which puts less emphasis on iron play and more on putting. Fairways on most courses are getting wider. Pros hit the ball three hundred yards off the tee and leave themselves wedge shots to the green from the fairway or the rough—it ceases to matter. And to frost the cake, clubs are getting more "forgiving." Bottom line, Susan spends her time eating bon bons and watching the soaps on television. No one cares. Well, except Hesta, who now knows something she didn't before. Maybe this will change things. Stay tuned.

### What Susan Wants

Okay, since we're enlightened and telling the truth, here it goes. Susan would really like it if Phor would leave her alone. If he would just stop bothering her. No more calls, no more coming over unannounced, no more flowers delivered while she's thinking about really important things like if Marshall on *All My Children* will dump Celeste and marry Dirk, his secret lover.

## How to Become Susan's Friend

If you're a woman, no sweat. She's on your side. Which may not mean much, since she rarely pays attention to what you're doing. If you're male, Susan gets bored really fast. Think of a date when you were trying your utmost to impress the girl and getting nowhere, absolutely nowhere. The Pope would have a better chance of getting to first base. Now make it a hundred times worse. That is one-tenth of how bad it is with Susan. Male or female, if you want Susan to help you with accuracy during a round, briefly, and I mean briefly, think a thought of how nice and helpful she is, then quickly think of something else. Then, think of how charming she is, very briefly, and then think of something else. Say her name under your breath. "Susan, what a lovely name." Then sigh. Wait a minute before hitting. Who knows? She may help, she may not.

## Guardian Golf God Pledge

*I solemnly swear that I will provide men and women, girls and boys, the ability to hit a golf ball where you are aiming if at all possible.*

## A Sampling of Current or Former Guardian Clients

Natalie Gulbis, Professional golfer
Pat Hurst, Professional golfer
Fred Funk, Professional golfer
Calvin Peete, Professional golfer
Bill Clinton, U.S. President
Charles Gibson, TV news anchor

# Otom

## *Area of Responsibility*

Pride

## *Golf God Level*

Major-Minor (stable at this time between golf god levels.)

## *Biography*

Very early in his tenure as a golf god, Phor noticed how difficult the game was. He watched players struggle to get the ball airborne, to hit it the right distance, even to hit the ball. Golf, he saw, was a diabolically cruel game. Yet even the worst players returned to play again. He wondered what this trait was that kept golfers trying and trying again to achieve even the smallest measures of success.

While walking a course one winter afternoon contemplating this interesting aspect of the game he noticed a large oak tree, bare of leaves except for one that still hung on far out on a branch. He watched as this one leaf was buffeted by winter winds, refusing to let go of its summer perch. Why would a leaf cling so dearly to what was and not venture on to what might be? Was it fear? Was it stubbornness? Was this one leaf somehow not finished being a leaf?

He made it a point to walk by this tree and this leaf every day. No matter how fiercely the night winds might blow, on every walk he could see the dried-out brown-and-yellow leaf holding fast to the branch.

"Leaf," he said one day. "I see you are a leaf of some distinction. I admire your steadfastness. I wonder why you are doing as you do just as I wonder and am, in fact, in awe of what my golfers endure. I believe you may understand what I am only beginning to be aware of. Would you become a golf god? I admit not knowing of what at this moment, but I am sure you will know." Sensing acceptance in the fabric of entities Phor made the leaf a golf god.

*Otom*

Now named Otom, the leaf said it was pride in being a leaf that kept him from loosening his grip on the tree. "And I do believe," he added, "that pride is also what drives the true golfer to endure what must be endured to be a golfer."

Pride for Otom is not so much in the results for the golfer, the pride a person finds in victory. Otom's emphasis is the pride the golfer has in the game that requires so much from the player: pride in always trying hard when reward is so rare; pride in overcoming adversity; pride in taking care of the game; pride in playing by the rules and honoring opponents; pride in doing the right thing no matter what the personal cost.

Not surprisingly, Otom has a bit of a nasty side, as befits a leaf that would be stubborn enough to hang on a branch long beyond the time it was supposed to let go. Otom loves sensing false pride in a golfer and sticking it to him. Believe you're one notch better than you are and he'll help you be four notches worse. Ignorance is just about as noxious to Otom as false pride. Believe your ball doesn't make a pitch mark in the green? Don't bother to look? Otom is watching, and Otom will "educate" you in ways that you won't recognize, but you sure won't like.

### What Otom Wants

The golf god of pride wants you to be humble. Recognize that you are one of 50,000,000 golfers in a game enjoyed and revered around the world. In the grand scheme of golf you are a very small part. Yet, like a leaf on a tree, you are an important part of the whole. Recognize that everything you do can contribute to our grand old game or, conversely, detract from it.

### How to Become Otom's Friend

Accept without reservation that golf is the fairest game on earth. Believe that your role in golf is to try your hardest, enjoy yourself and your playing companions, take care of the course and game as you play, and protect the game for future players. As you play and things get tough, visualize that oak leaf hanging on, never giving up, being the best darn leaf it can be—and do the same for yourself.

### Guardian Golf God Pledge

*I'm your guy if you're having trouble with your temper, if you have too fast a swing, a negative attitude at the first hint of trouble, and a tendency to try low-percentage shots. I can help you through good times and bad. Tiger liked the idea of never giving up, and has asked me to be his guardian golf god quite a few times.*

### A Sampling of Current or Former Guardian Clients

Tiger Woods, Professional golfer
Chris DiMarco, Professional golfer
Ben Hogan, Professional golfer, legend
JoAnne Carner, Professional golfer
Joe Louis Barrow, Executive Director, First Tee
Colin Powell, U.S. Army General

# Nogoeh

### Area of Responsibility

Protecting par

### Golf God Level

Major-Minor (used to be a Major)

### Biography

Nogoeh, his original and current name, was a spirit to a group of Native Americans on the northwestern shores of Hudson Bay. He was called on for compassion and safety when the men would go out among the ice floes seeking seals, and on occasion walruses and polar bears. However, since he was a vegetarian, this duty was difficult for him to perform. When Phor was recruiting golf gods, Nogoeh immediately applied. He was charged with protecting par.

As he defined his responsibilities there were two elements: protecting par on each hole and protecting par for an entire round of golf. He knew that golf would be boring if all eighteen holes were equally difficult. Variety was important, so he didn't obsess about par being hard to get on every hole. The intricacies of risk/reward became important.

In the hunting society for which he was an important spirit, risking a harpoon was a serious matter. Too massive a target or an inaccurate throw could cost a valuable tool. Decisions were made on a three-point scale. An assessment of cost/benefit that rated a one was a no-go, too much chance for too little gain. A two was when food was scarce and a chance should be taken. A three was a no-brainer, toss the darn thing. Nogoeh has since inspired golfers and golf architects to have a similar set of thoughts as they go about their respective tasks; too many decisions, not fun, too few decisions, no challenge. Next time you play, see if you experience a good blend of decision opportunities. This was Nogoeh's way of making hole-by-hole par interesting.

His task was a bit different over eighteen holes. He wanted par to be a difficult goal to reach, but not so difficult that it seemed impossible to many golfers. Here, he was brilliant. He knew that most golfers would think, "If I can par five holes in a round, why not par eighteen—or at least average par for all eighteen?" The closer a player gets to this goal the more golden the goal becomes.

For a considerable period, post-1900 and well into the 1940s, par even for the ablest golfers was a rewarding achievement. Bob Jones often remarked that his intent when playing matches was to continue throwing "Old Man Par" at his opponent. He meant, of course, Nogoeh. A tour professional who averaged par every round in those days would take home a considerable amount of prize money.

Unfortunately, today par is becoming old fashioned. Old Man Par is simply an old man, at least at the professional level. The only people who seem to still revere him are those folks at the USGA.

Yet on the daily-fee courses Nogoeh still reigns supreme. Turn in a card that equals par and you'll win everything. Turn in a card with all pars and you won't have to buy a drink for months. Just like survival in the Arctic exacted just about everything a body had, so does matching par for the average Joe, for a hole, two in a row, or the more exalted round of par for nine or the complete eighteen.

### What Nogoeh Wants

He'd like making a par to equal the satisfaction that everyone has after taking on a difficult task and being successful. He is not interested in making par almost impossible, a mistake he hopes the USGA will quit making. However, he is interested in making par a more satisfying experience than what you currently read on the face of a tour pro that has just made one. Scoring under par should be a rewarding time, not an entitlement just because you can play well.

### How to Become Nogoeh's Friend

This is about the easiest thing in the world to do. Nogoeh has wonderful perspective on the game. He knows without doubt that golf is not life or death. He knows of life and death in

*Nogoeh*

the harshest habitable environment. Golf is a game played in a park. But he knows that a game without challenge is boring. You can please Nogoeh by approaching golf as an enjoyable and challenging game, one where success is measured in part by scoring par on a hole. Greater success is enjoyed by scoring par for the round, and even greater success for making par on every hole. When you par a hole, let Nogoeh know that you understand you have succeeded at this little game, that you appreciate the effort necessary to make par, and that you are thankful to be playing such a special game. A mental "Thank you" every once in a while is sufficient.

If you're able to do at least some of these things Nogoeh will not help you play any better, for scoring really isn't the point.

He, more than anyone else, recognizes the delicious challenge that golf offers: of you against yourself. However, if you learn to appreciate par, he'll make sure that when you get one or two or more, or even score under par, that you will experience the same joy, contentment, and perspective as the early Native Americans when they brought down a magnificent beast with the honor it deserved.

### Guardian Golf God Pledge

*As a number par means nothing. As a symbol of golf mastery nothing is its equal. Honor the concept by asking me to be your guardian golf god. I will increase your golf wisdom tenfold. And if you think more than you swing I'll help you to climb the mountain.*

### A Sampling of Current or Former Guardian Clients

Bob Jones IV, Amateur golfer
Donald Trump, Deal maker
USGA, Entire executive committee
Willie Nelson, Musician
Johnny Depp, Actor
Harold W. McGraw III, Businessman

# The Minor Golf Gods

| | |
|---|---|
| CHIT | TERRNOR |
| POKKIE | FAUNIS |
| FABU | WOODA |
| UNULIGT | BACYSOS |

These are Minor golf gods in rank only. Don't be fooled into thinking they are unimportant and should be ignored. Just as a 300-yard drive and a 3-inch putt count the same on a scorecard, the minor golf gods are every bit as involved in your game as the others.

You've heard the saying "The devil is in the details"? The minor golf gods made that one up. They look out for the small things in your game, the details that can be overlooked but that can contribute so much to your enjoyment. Take breaking a hundred for the first time as an example. The difference between 105 and 104 is only one stroke, just as the difference between 100 and 99 is just one stroke, but what a huge difference in meaning. Fabu is in charge of that small number and is intensely interested in having you experience what that number means.

Unuligt, the golf god of a perfect game, is not going to be of much benefit to most golfers who have trouble driving to the course let alone hitting drives on the course. But at the same time, a nod of the cap to Unuligt could improve your game quite a bit.

Each of the minor golf gods will have something of importance to offer you. It is up to you to appreciate what that is and to appreciate them.

# Chit

## Area of Responsibility

Bunkers

## Golf God Level

Minor (but not minor to most golfers)

## Biography

Chit is a macho golf god. He was spontaneously created by the thought processes of the other golf gods, who were enamored of the sound players made when they either found themselves in the sand or had trouble getting the ball out of the sand. He is named after that sound. He is young by golf god standards but is fully in control of his powers.

Although a minor golf god Chit can cause considerable harm to a golf score. His favorite place in the world is the Road Hole bunker on the seventeenth hole at the Old Course in St. Andrews. During the third round of the 1978 Open Championship, Tommy Nakajima was playing the seventeenth hole within a few strokes of the lead. His ball was just off the green in two. Sadly, he let himself think that the dastardly Road Hole bunker was now impotent. You should never think something is impotent, especially a young male golf god.

Nakajima's twenty-five-yard shot to the hole was sucked into the bunker. It could go nowhere else. Then the trouble began. Chit made him hit the first shot too softly. The ball came out, then rolled back in. Chit made the same thing happen a second time. Then a third time. Nakajima's hubris evaporated, and on his fourth effort from the sand Chit allowed the ball to come out.

## What Chit Wants

Despite his relative youth, Chit believes that golf has become too easy, especially after Gene Sarazen invented the sand wedge, and with the growing popularity and use of lob wedges. Chit wants players to respect the difficulty of golf, even to the point of preferring the game to be hard rather than easy. He wants you to believe that bunkers add to the game. He will be yours forever if you believe that bunkers have become too easy and that perhaps they should no longer be raked.

Recently, Chit influenced Jack Nicklaus to make the bunkers more punitive at the 2006 Memorial tournament. Jack misunderstood the idea and only removed a few teeth from the bunker rakes. Chit wanted him to remove the rakes all the way to the trash bin.

### How to Become Chit's Friend

At the very least you have to truly believe that bunkers are an interesting, even a welcome challenge. Other things you could do are: carry only two wedges, rake the sand but tell your playing companions that the game might be better if bunkers weren't raked, appreciate the placement of bunkers, practice bunker shots, and educate yourself on the different kinds of sand.

He also appreciates it if, when you yell out his name, you do it so it sounds like you're enjoying yourself. For example, if you see your ball heading toward a bunker, yell "Chit" as if you were hailing a good friend. If you swing and the ball remains in the bunker, yell "Chit" in a way that thanks him for the extra challenge. He loves having his name make a positive impact on the game. So yell it loud and yell it proud.

If you take more than two swings to extricate yourself from a bunker, somehow you have offended Chit. Whenever this occurs you must clean your sand wedge, including washing the grip, and tell Chit you're sorry. You will be back in his good graces immediately.

### Guardian Golf God Pledge

*I will reduce the number of bunkers (sand or otherwise) you are in by 30 percent and reduce your total number of bunker shots by another 30 percent. In addition, you will hole out from a bunker (sand or otherwise) five times during every season I am your guardian golf god.*

## *A Sampling of Current or Former Guardian Clients*

Tsuneyuki Nakajima, Professional golfer
Birdie Kim, Professional golfer
Bob Tway, Professional golfer
Sandy Lyle, Professional golfer
Paul Azinger, Professional golfer
Richard Karn, Actor

# Terrnor

## Area of Responsibility

Water

## Golf God Level

Minor (on the fast track to become a Major-Minor golf god)

## Biography

At the time she became a golf god Terrnor was a middle-aged bluegill *(lepomis macrohirus)* living near the western shores of Lake Michigan. She had just deposited 44,000 eggs and was quite exhausted when the call to golf goddom arrived.

Dupta, the original golf god of water, was a hothead. He wielded his opinion like a club, banging it off the heads of the other golf gods. Some of the golf gods thought he was self-righteous, while others hoped he would simply dry up and go away.

Water, Dupta felt, should be surprising, absolute, and most importantly, rare. He regretted the proliferation of artificial lakes and other water features on modern designer courses. "Let the water lie almost unnoticed while the golfer plays over and around it a thousand times. When the water wins once it will plague him forever," was Dupta's idea.

He admired the Swilkin Burn at the St. Andrews Old Course. The only water hazard in play on this venerated course is no more than a ditch narrow enough to leap across. Although it runs immediately in front of the first green it rarely comes into play. Topped shots from the fairway have been known to bound over it as if it didn't exist. Its very inconsequence is what makes it such a powerful hazard. Having a ball come to rest in it is such a shock on the very first hole that the player must regroup before even having a chance to group.

Watching the Tournament Players Championship, Dupta observed many of the best golfers in the world plopping into the drink on the seventeenth hole's island green. Then and there he decided to give up being the golf god of water. "They want water," he said, "I'll give them water." He closed his eyes and visualized fish. The first one in view was this female bluegill in Lake Michigan. He immediately bestowed upon her all his golf god powers, named her Terrnor, left, and hasn't been seen since.

The effect on Terrnor was indescribable. In an instant she went from a decimal-point intelligence, barely being able to sense heat and cold, to having an IQ that soared into the high 10,000s. Since she doesn't have fingers, she can't use a computer like most of the other golf gods. Not being able to take notes means she cannot keep track of things as well as the other golf gods, either. Thus she may forget that she wanted to help you, and equally may forget she wanted to make you pay for a transgression.

### What Terrnor Wants

Her philosophy, following Dupta's, is that water is for fish and other aquatic life, not intended as a feature on a golf course. She wants courses to contain the absolute least amount of water possible, preferably in ponds rather than lakes, preferably in streams rather than ponds, preferably in a natural meandering stream rather than a design feature taking center stage.

If a player hits into a water hazard, the response should be shock, not anger. The golfer should become aware that the water was always lying quietly, waiting the golfer's misstep. Water is not a bully or a cold slap in the face but a natural part of the landscape. If the ball ends up wet, she wants the golfer to accept responsibility.

### How to Become Terrnor's Friend

Don't eat fish within ten days of playing a course with water on it. Don't casually toss a ball into a water hazard and think you're "offering a ball to the gods." It's insulting. Terrnor has no need or desire for golf balls. If your ball goes into the water, say something like, "I screwed that one up," with a tone of acceptance. If you're foolish enough to play a designer course with lots of water, don't blame anyone but yourself. Think acceptance, and all will be well between you and Terrnor.

If you're facing a shot over water, the best chances of success lie in getting Terrnor's attention (she doesn't want golf balls

*Terrnor*

in her water, remember, any more than you do), then asking for help. Say "Terrnor, I need your help, please." Tee up a new ball to show your confidence in her and swing away.

If you got her attention you'll be fine. If your new ball goes into the drink, either you didn't get her attention or you have affronted her in some way. Don't eat fish or other seafood for a month.

### Guardian Golf God Pledge

*Choosing me for your golf god guardian will make you fearless with shots over water, increase by a factor of a hundred the number of times your ball will head toward water but hit a rock and land in the fairway, and lead you to success at least twice in your attempts to skip a shot over water and onto the green.*

### A Sampling of Current or Former Guardian Clients

Hale Irwin, Professional golfer
Davis Love III, Professional golfer
Ray Romano, Actor
Joe Hazelwood, Ship's captain
Tom Doak, Golf architect, writer
Geoff Shackelford, Golf architect, writer

# *Pokkie*

## *Area of Responsibility*

Pace of play

## *Golf God Level*

Minor

## *Biography*

In order to enhance his golf knowledge Phor had to travel through time to determine the true origin of golf. To do this he had to use a common but clever trick. You are probably aware of Einstein's formulation of $E = mc^2$. If you solve this equation for $c$, you get some of the idea of how much energy is necessary to accelerate a small amount of mass to very high speeds—not as much as you would think. For example, a simple flashlight accelerates a lot of light with a couple of D batteries. So the first part of time travel is to find a small enough mass to accelerate up to the speed of light, thereby slowing time for that particular mass to the point where time actually stops. This is simple enough to do. The trick is then to apply Newton's third law of motion, which states that every action involves an equal but opposite reaction.

What Phor did was to push the entire universe forward, the direction it is headed in anyway, reduce his mass to almost nothing, and then have Hesta push him backward as hard as she could. The result was that he accelerated to the speed of light, and the rest of the universe accelerated a little in the opposite direction, thus allowing his passage back in time.

Time travel isn't, as many people suppose, like watching a movie backward. It's more like a CD, on which you can stop anywhere and start up from there. You could stop at 500 years ago, go to 20 years ago, then go back 300 years. There is no need to do things in any sequence, and you can always get back to your starting point. Going forward in time hasn't been done yet, because to do so with current technology you'd have to get the entire universe to go backward while you went forward. This is harder to do than it sounds.

As you might guess, golf in the early days was played at a brisk pace, partly because it was more often played in winter than summer. On the warmer days there was more outdoor work to be done. It was also a brisk pace because play was match play and holes didn't have to be completed to determine the winner, and because courses were often not much over 5,000 yards. Eighteen holes were played in about two hours.

While observing golf through time Phor was struck by how playing through a group in the olden days offered a moment of camaraderie. Players usually knew one another, had an idea of how each played, and were comfortable playing at whatever pace suited them and allowing those who wished to play faster to play through. As more people played and more courses became crowded with golfers unknown to one another, the event of playing through became an uncomfortable psychodrama, often ruining the rest of the game for all involved.

Upon his return from time travel, Phor decided to create an opening for a golf god of pace of play in order to keep golf a walk in the park rather than a laborious trudge, and to take some control over the difficult golfing intersection of playing through. To find a new golf god, he decided to look over the list kept in heaven of those wishing to become one. There was one fellow who appeared most appropriate for this new position.

In life, the man had been a common soldier in the 1950–53 Korean War. This 1,127-day conflict left an estimated five million dead, half of them civilians. He died early in the war during the battle at Chosin, a reservoir deep in North Korea. It was war at its worst, numbing cold, little or no food, with the constant barrage of big guns and the horror of hand-to-hand combat. Attacks were constant. No one could sleep for more than a couple of hours at a time. There were no tents, and often the nighttime temperature dropped to forty below. Food was frozen. Feet were frozen. Many soldiers froze to death overnight.

Phor chose a man who was wounded by mortar fire one morning on a rocky hillside. His legs were a mass of blood, as was his left arm. The cold was slowly seeping through his extremities to his core but did little to dull pain that was all but unbearable. He knew he was dying. All he could do was lie and watch as occasional small arms skirmishes were waged nearby.

He was married, had two children, and back home worked on a farm. He smiled as he thought of his family. It had been a good life. They would be taken care of when he did not return. He wished he could die with a bit more dignity rather than lying sprawled on a hillside. He had fired his gun only a few times, not really aiming, not really wishing to hit anyone. It was a war he didn't understand.

Just before nightfall, when he knew the dark and cold would again make him feel desperately alone, there was a sound of falling rocks above him. A soldier slid down next to him. An enemy soldier. They looked at one another, expressionless. One was helpless; one was fully armed. Neither spoke the other's language; neither tried to talk.

The enemy examined the man's wounds, shook his head, and then looked in the other man's eyes. The enemy soldier reached to his waist, undid his holster, and pulled out his revolver. Expressionless, he handed it to his enemy.

When the pain became too great, Korean Army Private Chong used this gift of choice to end his life after saying a prayer for his family, thanking the American soldier, and straightening himself out as well as he could.

While in heaven, Chong became an Arnold Palmer fan. He fell in love with a game he never played (on earth) and wished so very much he could get involved somehow. So, he put his name on the waiting list, and Phor thought he would be perfect for the new position of overseeing pace of play and, of course, playing through.

### What Pokkie Wants

Pokkie wants, more than anything, honor among players. His wartime experience and the compassionate act of the American soldier taught him the importance of respect no matter what the differences. When the situation arises when one group plays through another one, differences are both obvious and assumed.

Neither, Pokkie thinks, should affect play or the players. Should it matter that the faster group is faster? No. That they may be more skillful, younger, better looking, wealthier, etc.? No, no, no, and no.

Pokkie also wants this situation to occur more often. It seems that as courses become more crowded, fewer groups allow faster ones through. "No place to go," they think, so the faster groups end up stewing in the fairway for hours until darkness demands they abandon the round.

### How to Become Pokkie's Friend

Don't wait until an entire hole opens up ahead of you. Let others through as soon as you realize you won't keep up. Anticipate a good time to let a group play through and let them know beforehand so they can be prepared. Tell the players following that you will wave them up to hit to the green before you putt out, for example.

Pokkie loves it when players remind each other to play efficiently. He also likes seeing the group allowing the faster group through place themselves as far from the tee as possible, minimizing the audience. As the faster group finishes and is about to move on, a gracious "Play well" pleases Pokkie immensely.

Golf is a game of movement. A slow pace of play disappoints him. Pokkie is not the kind of golf god to make a statement by creating problems for you on the course. Not directly, anyway. His technique is to make his point by affecting who your golfing companions are. The more you neglect this area of golf etiquette, the less appealing your golf companions will become. Next time you play, notice who your companions are; think how long it really takes you to play a round; recall if players behind you have to stand and wait before hitting their shots; and see if you're wise enough to understand the connection. Of course, Pokkie does his best to make the opposite happen too.

You should remember that Pokkie is extremely concerned about what people think. When you play through, any misgivings you feel are thoughts put in your head by Pokkie trying to help. Acknowledge them and then forget them. If tension causes you to top the ball don't get mad at Pokkie,* he's doing his best.

Also realize that Pokkie's mental condition is sometimes an asset if not taken to the extreme. He is always thinking about how a player's behavior on the course affects other golfers. When he keeps things in perspective, he is a great steward of the game. He'd like you to be one too.

Aside from Pokkie's fixation on pace of play and playing through, these are the top five things you can do to foster his best wishes and his interest in helping you play well:

- Learn how to manage your equipment so you can minimize its effect on playing time: Leave your clubs in the direction that you'll go when you leave the green, for instance, or if you ride a cart, don't put your club back in your bag until you're ready to pick out the next one.
- Figure out what you want to do before it's your turn to hit.
- Play the tees that best fit your game.
- Play less stroke play and more match play—picking up when you're out of a hole.
- Take fewer swings.

### Guardian Golf God Pledge

*Nothing is more important than your reputation. If you choose me as your guardian golf god I will make sure you are the first called when someone is putting together a game. I also promise that as an invitee you will play golf for free at least seven times while I am your guardian golf god. However, none of this will happen if you don't invite golfers to play through as appropriate, or if you chronically play at the pace of a slug. Please, life is short; take care of one another.*

---

* It has to be said at this point that there is no documentation of these Korean War events. However, it is without doubt that somehow or other Pokkie's problem with paranoia and a dysfunctional corpus callosum or whatever it is continues to make playing through a major trauma for him and thus for most golfers.

*A Sampling of Current or Former Guardian Clients*

Rory Sabbatini, Professional golfer
Amy Sabbatini, Spouse
Fultom Allem, Professional golfer
Ben Crane, Professional golfer
Lanny Wadkins, Professional golfer
Nick Faldo, TV Commentator

# *Faunis*

*Area of Responsibility*

Ball on a tee

*Golf God Level*

Minor

*Biography*

In the early days of golf, tees were unheard of. Players simply dropped a ball on the first teeing ground and began play. After holing out they would drop the ball within two club lengths of the hole and keep going. On March 9, 1673, on the nine-hole course near Forres in Scotland, Ian Gaintree dropped his ball on the ground after holing out on the third. Instead of swinging at the ball however, he stared at it. The ball sat on the grass as it always had, but Ian was thinking.

He was thinking about how casual they all were. Drop the ball and hit it. In his mind these rare occasions that allowed the player to touch the ball should be more carefully considered. During play balls in ruts, balls in sewers, balls under rocks all had to be played as they lay. Special clubs were designed to extract errant balls from all sorts of messes. But players were allowed to reach into the hole to get the ball, then drop it nearby. This benefit should be taken advantage of.

Ian decided to place his ball on a tuft of grass and set it up just a bit. This worked very well when there was adequate grass. Later, when there wasn't adequate grass nearby, one fateful day, he pulled together a small pile of dirt with his fingers and placed his ball on top. After doing this a number of times and with a bit of experimentation, he learned that a pinch of wet sand made the best platform for his ball. Other players, of course, saw what he was doing, noticed how it improved his opening shot, and quickly began creating their own small piles of sand.

Strangers to this part of Scotland noticed, too. When they first saw him put together the sandy pile they asked him what he was doing. "I'm teaing the ball," he would answer. He called it "teaing" because the pinch of sand reminded him of a clump of tea leaves. Strangers then began "teeing" (modern spelling) the ball just like Ian. This trend slowly grew until almost every golfer worldwide teed off by creating a small mound of sand or dirt, placing the ball on top, and swinging away. Lady and gentlemen players, of course, had their caddies perform this task.

All was fine and natural until an American came into the picture thinking he could somehow improve on this well-established practice. A Harvard Dental School graduate by the name of George Grant invented the first wooden golf tee in 1896. Why he did this is anyone's guess, but it may be he was seeking a more

*Faunis*

positive public image than he got extracting teeth with pliers or drilling into cavities with a 180 rpm drill. Even though dentist Grant had the patent it took another dentist (one has to wonder), this time William Lowell of New Jersey, to mass-produce and mass-market the tiny wooden wonders. By 1921 everyone who played stored a handful of dime-a-dozen tees in a pocket of the golf bag.

Phor saw the implications immediately. This artificial device on the playing grounds could be the beginning of many more artificial devices to come. Golf was headed in a critical and totally negative direction as far as he was concerned. The game was supposed to be a walk across the countryside, man and nature, not an exercise of lugging a golf bag stuffed with half a dozen high-tech golfers' aids. He went to his list of minor gods who were looking for a new god gig and found Faunis, the former god of cod fishing for a small group of villagers on the southwest coast of Iceland. Faunis immediately accepted the assignment of making it difficult to rest a ball on top of a wooden peg. Alas, in spite of her best efforts to blow the ball off a million and one tees, baking the ground too hard to pound one deep enough to stay upright, chipping the edges of the tee so the ball would roll off, and anything else she could think of, today's golfer couldn't begin to conceive of the old-fashioned alternative of playing the ball off the ground from beginning to end.

If she wanted to, Faunis could knock the ball off everyone's tee for the next ten years and not tire one bit. But she realizes that she has lost the battle. She doesn't want to make things difficult for golfers.

### What Faunis Wants

Faunis wants golfers to appreciate what they have. Nowhere else on the course do you have complete control over the golf ball. She wants people to take advantage of this accidental and not-so-positive element of golf. Tee up smart. Place the lettering on the ball along your intended swing path, or, alternatively, place the name at the back of the ball as it rests on the tee as the target for the club. You could even place the name toward the inside if you wanted to hit a draw or the outside to hit more of a cut shot. Place the name near the bottom to encourage a sweeping swing. Tee the ball lower to hit a slice, higher for a draw. Tee the ball on one side of the tee box or the other depending on the shape of your shot, and to hit away from any trouble in the fairway.

### How to Become Faunis's Friend

Don't take anything for granted. Take your time on the tee to figure out how to best take advantage of this unique situation. Don't leave broken tees lying around. Dispose of them so they don't become hazards for the mowers or an eyesore for following players. If you hit an especially good tee shot say something like, "Faunis, thank you, old girl." She loves that. She was close to retiring when those three-pronged plastic tees came out, the ones that looked like a thin, three-legged spider engaged in a difficult bowel movement. She appreciates anyone using a simple wooden peg. Don't buy or use anything fancy.

### Guardian Golf God Pledge

*If I am honored as your choice to be your guardian golf god, I pledge that you will have eighteen perfect lies in the fairway during every round in addition to your eighteen tee shots. (This pledge does not apply to any professional golfer or tournament golf other than scramble-format during a charity event.)*

### A Sampling of Current or Former Guardian Clients

Barbara Asperger, Beginning golfer
Denelle Reilly, Amateur golfer
John Elway, Football player
Tom Cruise, Actor
Peter Dawson, Golf administrator
Dent-de-Lion du Midi, Inventor

# *Fabu*

### *Area of Responsibility*

Breaking 100

### *Golf God Level*

Minor (although many believe she should be a major golf god)

### *Biography*

Fabu owes her existence to the demise of match play and the interest, especially in the United States, of playing stroke play and counting all one's swings until the bitter end. Hesta is the one who thought up the benefit of having a golf god of breaking 100.

Somewhere in the late 1950s or maybe the early '60s Hesta observed the high number of players who struggled to score in the double digits for eighteen holes. Breaking that barrier became a symbol, different for different players. Young players saw it as a slowly approaching milestone of golf maturity, men golfers defined it as final mastery of the game, while women for the most part deemed it an impossible dream.

In conceptualizing the role of a golf god for breaking 100 Hesta had a few characteristics in mind. She wanted the barrier to be psychologically approachable yet profound. Scoring 99 or less should be a strong cause for celebration. She also wanted such a feat to be memorable; the player should remember some of the shots, playing companions, the course, maybe even all the details of the last three or four holes. She wanted children to most easily break the barrier, men to struggle, and women to be taken almost by surprise the first time they accomplished this glorious feat.

Hesta searched the list of out-of-work minor gods and didn't find anyone suitable. She then took a look at the list of those in heaven looking for more action. One name, that of a shepherd girl from a remote area of present-day Iran, stood out. The name had been listed for almost 500 years. This girl had died just as she was entering adolescence, drowned trying to save one of her flock. Her dedication was just what Hesta was looking for. When asked, the girl immediately accepted her new role.

Hesta transfigured the girl into human form for about six months during the early 1960s so she could try out the game and better understand its players. Hesta named her Judy for her earthly existence, and Judy didn't have to plead much to be made twenty-five and beautiful. She played at the Dearborn Hills Country Club just outside Detroit. Here she learned what we all know. Kids play golf mostly for fun; men play for the competition and the fellowship; women play for the fellowship and to do something out of the ordinary. Women golfers, Judy decided, don't much care if they ever break 100 unless they become competitive players. Men, on the other hand, are desperate to break 100 at least once in their golfing lifetimes. Kids that stick with the game just assume it's only a matter of time.

### What Fabu Wants

Judy, who became the golf god Fabu upon her return from earthly form, had a clear idea of her role. It was exactly what Hesta had in mind. Kids would be helped to grow step by step into the pleasures of breaking 100. Men would sweat bullets, tremble over putts, and watch their chances go down the drain countless times before being accepted into the exclusive club. Female social golfers would not care a whit if they ever broke 100.

Fabu wants these categories of golfers to accept their fate with dignity. She will help those she thinks deserve help and hinder those she thinks are undeserving.

### How to Become Fabu's Friend

If you're a kid, don't sweat it. She is mostly a kid and is totally on your side. Relax and enjoy the journey. If you're a male golfer, don't get mad if you approach oh-so-close to breaking 100, then miss the mark. Fabu is testing you. If you miss by a stroke or two, especially at the very end, tip your hat to the grand lady and say, "Fabu, you're fabulous," and visualize some movie starlet you think she might look like. If you're a woman golfer and you care if you break 100, practice, especially your short game, and Fabu will help you all she can. Just say "Thanks" to her when you do the deed.

### Guardian Golf God Pledge

*If you haven't broken 125 yet I suggest you have Bok, Bango, or Bongo for your guardian golf god first. Once you're shooting close to 110 or lower make me your guardian golf god and I'll make sure you break through the first season we're together.*

### A Sampling of Current or Former Guardian Clients

Dwight Eisenhower, U.S. President
Bill Gates, World health and education patron
Cameron Diaz, Actress
Kelsey Grammer, Actor
Arnold Schwarzenegger, Governor (California)
Rob Prouty, Amateur golfer

# *Wooda*

### *Area of Responsibility*

First tee

### *Golf God Level*

Minor

### *Biography*

In 1927 Suzanne Lilliquest of Scranton, Pennsylvania, was resting on her front porch on a humid August night. She was sipping lemonade trying to keep cool, half-listening to the distant trills of crickets and thinking about how soon her husband would be home from the afternoon shift at the butterball factory. Suzanne didn't know it yet, but she was pregnant with her first child. As she sat daydreaming on the porch swing, deep rumbling began in the west, signaling the approach of yet another summer thunderstorm. Flashes of lightning became brighter, the thunder louder and more immediate. She could feel the storm coming closer.

The crack of thunder was almost deafening. Rain would pour down at any moment. As she got up to go into the house lightning struck one of the horseshoe stakes in the front yard, traveled along the hose she had left out that morning, jumped up the steps of the porch, and knocked her flat.

The next day the newspaper said it was a miracle she lived, let alone suffered absolutely no injuries. At least that's what they thought at the time. When her child was born nine months later they learned the truth. Everything about Phillip Ross Lilliquest was normal except that he was missing the appendage that would truly qualify him to be a Phillip as opposed to a Phyllis. Trouble was, he didn't look exactly like a Phyllis either. He was a mystery for a few hours until it was clear that what normal humans needed two to do, he did with one.

Examinations, X-rays, and a little delicate prodding determined that the equipment he (using the term very loosely) had would work fine but it was clear that neither a he nor a she would he ever be.

In spite of his unusual start, PR Lilliquest lived as normal a life as anyone could growing up in Scranton, Pennsylvania, in the 1930s. Just before World War II the family, now consisting of dad, mom, and three children, moved to Nebraska. It was here that PR fell in love with music, jazz music that he heard over the radio. He worked long hours at the Pic and Pay grocery and earned enough to buy a beat-up old Gibson guitar. Most evenings he'd be out by the barn picking on that guitar and enthusiastically singing to himself.

PR didn't have a clue then about his ears. They were big, really big, huge; everybody noticed that. But to them and to PR they were just big ears. No one had an inkling of what they were really for.

When PR was seventeen and ready to graduate from high school, and after playing the guitar and singing to himself for thousands of hours out by the barn, he made his public debut at the high school talent show. He chose a jazz number that was mostly strumming with just a bit of singing. When he played the guitar there was polite listening. When he sang the few words of the song there was considerable heavy breathing, a few sighs, and a significant amount of wiggling around, especially in the front rows. Boys and girls hopped up to him after the show, insisting, even begging him to sing more.

So he did, at the malt shop that evening. This time he sang a song with a lot of words. With each verse the crowd jiggled and wiggled more. There was moaning and groaning. Boys started hugging the girls. Girls started jumping on the boys. Wrestling matches broke out. Clothes were ripped off. Pandemonium ensued. The police were called and broke it up.

Then PR got an invite to sing on the radio. That's when the governor and the judge came by the house and told him he wasn't allowed to sing in Nebraska any more.

PR stopped singing—in public anyway. He got a regular job, went on a few dates that never led to anything. By this time his ears were enormous, elephant-like, too much for any girl to overlook. He was turned down by the army because they couldn't overlook his ears either. They figured he'd be bad for morale,

*Wooda*

maybe not even be able to run to attack the enemy—too much wind resistance. He set up his life in Colby, Nebraska, as assistant to the manager of the Tapestry Bakery. He played golf in the nine-hole municipal league and was as happy as a man could be living in central Nebraska.

In the mid-1960s his doctor told him about a scientific institute in Southern California that might want to take a look at his unusual plumbing. He went down there and gave a lot of blood, endured a lot of tests, and answered a lot of questions. This is what they told him.

"Mr. Lilliquest, you are a very unusual man. Ah, in fact, you are not a man but not a woman either. We tested your sex chromosomes, you know the Xs and Ys that make up the two sexes. We didn't find any. What we found were two Zs, shaped almost like lightning bolts. You don't have any Xs or Ys. You're a completely different sex. You're a third sex."

It took a while for PR to digest this news. When he did, they told him some more.

"Once we determined you were a sex unto yourself we explored just how reproduction could take place. It's your ears, Mr. Lilliquest, and your voice. Your singing and listening are your sex's sexual organs. Singing and listening to singing are like having sex. That's why your singing had the kids out of control."

PR went home. One thought he had was that it was lucky he didn't go blind with all that singing out by the barn.

Phor heard about PR Lilliquest and had to hear for himself. He made himself invisible and listened one morning while PR was singing in the shower. The effect on the top golf god was considerable. "We have to have this PR around," he said to himself. There was nothing Phor loved more than robust singing.

Phor made himself visible, startling the heck out of PR. They sat and discussed their mutual interests. Phor made PR an offer.

"I'm as happy as a man can be living in central Nebraska," PR said. "But I sure think it would be more enjoyable to be a golf god."

So Phor made him one. The name "Wooda" came from their mutual admiration of Woody Herman.

### What Wooda Wants

Wooda wants all players to be totally confident before play begins, to anticipate an enjoyable day, and to have warmly greeted the day's playing companions. And he wants for there to be a song in everyone's heart.

### How to Become Wooda's Friend

Don't begin the round making excuses for how you might play that day. Don't mention sore backs, long nights, hurt wrists, or how long it's been since you last swung a club. Do wish your playing companions good luck. To especially tickle Wooda after you put the ball on the tee, tug on your ear like Carol Burnett used to do on her television show. That will crack him up.

To get Wooda to pay special attention to you—in a good way—play jazz or the blues on your way to the course. You will be amazed at what he will do for your first tee shot.

### Guardian Golf God Pledge

*My pledge if you choose me as your guardian golf god is that you will never hit poorly off the first tee, no matter how nervous you may be. When you write my name on the scorecard, also draw a smiley face with ears, and all will be well.*

### A Sampling of Current or Former Guardian Clients

Morris Hatalski, Professional golfer, architect
Mao Zedong, Chairman, China
Ian Baker-Finch, Professional golfer, commentator
Bob Rotella, Golf psychologist
Bob Cullen, Golf writer
Alice Cooper, Rocker

# Umuligt

*Area of Responsibility*

Shooting 54

*Golf God Level*

Minor (most minor golf god)

*Biography*

Umuligt was a totally unimportant Swedish god a long way down in the hierarchy of Norse gods. In the old days of the Vikings, Umuligt (then named Obe) was the god of raisin toast. This was a god position because raisins were a rare commodity in those days and in those regions, and even more rarely baked in bread. Moreover, he was a minor god because only a couple of villages made toast once the bread with raisins in it was baked.

Yet Obe was a contented god. He was thought of and thanked just the right amount for someone who was bashful in the spotlight. He would just as soon have been the god of raisin toast as any other god. "Just let me be and I will be there for thee," was his mantra. He never let anyone down. If someone had raisin toast and gave thanks to Obe he would bless them with good luck for at least a month.

As modern times arrived, any kind of bread could be found on grocery shelves, and most households owned toasters, Obe had less and less to do. He could have had more to do, actually, if he had promoted giving thanks for raisin toast, since it had become popular in a lot of places, but he was still a reclusive guy and preferred to let things be.

A little-known law about minor gods, however, interrupted his laid-back approach to being a god. It was written and agreed to long ago that for a minor god to remain a god, that minor god had to be revered by a certain percentage of the local population and at minimum frequency, and had to do something at least once a month for one or more of that god's believers. Obe really didn't want to be bothered, but he did like the life of being a god, especially a minor one. Again Phor came to the rescue of a god in trouble. He offered Obe the job of being the god of the perfect round of golf, a birdie on every hole. Even then, Obe had reservations.

"Do I have to be the golf god of the perfect round for the whole world?" he asked. Phor thought for a moment and said that he didn't. Next Obe asked, "If someone thinks about the perfect round and I make them feel just a little something, is that enough to count as a monthly effect?" Phor agreed to that too. So it was decided. Obe became Umuligt, the golf god of shooting a 54, almost exclusively for those with a connection to the country of Sweden.

### What Umuligt Wants

Pretty much to be left alone. To continue to exist as a golf god, however, at least one Swede a month must think about the possibility of shooting a 54 and feel at least some urge to do that someday.

### How to Become Umuligt's Friend

If you're a Swede or of Swedish descent, think about the wonder of a perfect round of golf every once in a while. There

*Umuligt*

is some chance that Umuligt will actually help you shoot a 54 if he feels there won't be too much of a fuss when you actually accomplish this feat.

If you're not Swedish or of Swedish descent, forget about Umuligt helping you to shoot a perfect round of golf; it will never happen. Or if it does, he will hear about it for the first time the next day and maybe send you a card. (Tiger Woods is not included in this discussion for obvious reasons, not excluding his rights by marriage.) Call on him for other things, however; he can help.

### Guardian Golf God Pledge

*I'm willing to help anyone in this order of priority: Swedes living in Sweden, Tiger Woods, Swedes living in Scandinavia, Swedes living anywhere else, Scandinavians living in Sweden, Scandinavians living outside of Sweden but somewhere in Scandinavia, Scandinavians living anywhere else, dead Swedes that have come back to life, people related by marriage to Swedes, everyone else.*

### A Sampling of Current or Former Guardian Clients

Tiger Woods, Professional golfer
Annika Sorenstam, Professional golfer
Pia Nilsson, Coach
Per-Ulrik Johansson, Professional golfer
Liselotte Neumann, Professional golfer
Fanny Sunesson, Caddie

# Bacysos

## Area of Responsibility

Holes in one

## Golf God Level

Minor

## Biography

The god Olokun was one of the progenitors of the Yoruba nation and is often considered the patron of Africans who were carried away from western Africa during the slave trade era. Olokun is the god of deep waters. Known for both female and male traits, Olokun is the personification of patience, endurance, and most especially wisdom.

Legend has it that Olokun suggested to Phor that golf needed a golf god of holes in one. His argument was that no one expects to make one, yet thousands are made every year. Additionally, those who manage the feat are momentarily stunned and ripe for an infusion of wisdom. It is a moment of euphoria and reflection that should be transformational.

Phor agreed and with Olokun's help chose Bacysos, a boy of nine who had died on one of the slave ships and whom Olokun had already invited to become one of the spirits of what is now modern-day Nigeria. As a boy, Bacysos was a prodigy able to predict storms and droughts, successfully ended a plague by cleaning up his village, and loved to look at the stars at night, once convincing the whole village to stay up all night to see a shower of meteors, which arrived just at the time he said they would. All that ended when the white men came and put irons on all the men of the village, taking them away in a long line of misery.

Olokun had sought a role for Bacysos that would best employ the boy's interest in science and at the same time promote some of his great insights. Bacysos was a great admirer of Ben Franklin and *Poor Richard's Almanac*. He loved nothing better than to wrap wisdom into a few words and tell them to everyone.

*Bacysos*

Bacysos was told that his responsibility was to decide who scored a hole in one and to inject the happy golfer with insight appropriate to the player. He relished the assignment.

### What Bacysos Wants

*Golf Digest* magazine once calculated the odds of an average golfer making a hole in one at about 12,000 to 1, depending on the length and difficulty of the hole and the relative skill of the golfer. Bacysos, who knows more about these things, places the actual odds at exactly 21,394.77 to 1. This means that for a golfer to have much of a chance to make a hole in one (since there are usually four par 3s on a course) he or she would have to play about 5,000 rounds, or a 100 rounds a year for fifty years. Not good enough odds for Bacysos.

He wants every golfer to make a hole in one so he can enlighten the lucky one with such gems he learned from Ben Franklin as:

- Experience keeps a dear school, but fools will learn in no other, and scarce in that.
- 'Tis easier to build two chimneys than to keep one in fuel.
- 'Tis hard for an empty bag to stand upright.
- Great estates may venture more, but little boats should keep near shore.
- When the well's dry, they know the worth of water.
- At a great pennyworth pause a while.
- Beware of little expenses; a small leak will sink a great ship.
- Industry need not wish.

### How to Become Bacysos's Friend

He would be delighted for you to make a hole in one. He has studied how and would like you to follow his advice.

Unless the green is extremely large or you're an extremely good player, aim for the center of the green no matter where the flagstick is. You will be on the green more often (it is almost impossible to score a hole in one if your ball is short, over, or to the side of the green). Take enough club to reach the center of the green and swing with confidence. You will be liked and admired by Bacysos; you'll score better on the par 3s; and, last but not least, you will reduce the odds of getting a hole in one to exactly 1,200 to 1.

### Guardian Golf God Pledge

*I strongly believe that every golfer who loves the game deserves to experience the rapture of scoring a hole in one. Therefore, when I am your guardian golf god, I pledge that if you aim for the center of the green on every par 3 you play, no matter where the flagstick is, I'll make sure that your ball will find the hole at least once.*

## *A Sampling of Current or Former Guardian Clients*

Paul Casey, Professional golfer
Scott Verplank, Professional golfer
Robert Mitera, Amateur golfer
Norman Manley, Amateur golfer
Harold Stilson, Amateur golfer
Jake Paine, Amateur golfer

# The Reverse Guide
# to the Golf Gods

Now that you are familiar with the golf gods you may find this reverse guide useful. Listed are common golf problems or situations. Find your problem, and you can look up what golf god may be of help and how you can get that help. Phor and Hesta are not listed. They can always be called upon for aid. If you have offended them, you may as well sell your clubs; no golf god will help you out.

Remember that the golf gods are just that. They are not workers or teachers or golf professionals. The difference between a golf instructor and a golf god is the same as the difference between a game of marbles and the solar system. You go to a professional golf teacher to help you cure a slice. You go to a golf god to help you get more out of playing golf. They will address what needs to be addressed, and it will not necessarily be what you think is the problem. They can do pretty much what they want, and your job is to encourage them to want to help you. You don't have to ask the golf god in charge of an area in order to get help in that area. Be creative, not demanding. The golf gods listed the five examples so that you could have an idea of how they operate. These are generalized; you can ask for help with specific issues, too, like pulling short putts or having difficulties with a specific hole at your usual course.

This list is by no means a complete guide for all problems. It offers just a few examples of how to approach a golf god. Remember, your golf problem is not the primary focus; the golf gods are.

| Problem or Situation | A Helpful Golf God | How to Ask for Help | Comments |
| --- | --- | --- | --- |
| Hitting a banana ball | Otom (Pride) | Say to Otom that you realize you are swinging too hard and too fast. Ask for help in appreciating a smooth swing. It would also be a good idea to play from tees more forward than you normally play for a while to show your good intentions. | Trying too hard to hit the ball is often the cause of a slice. Gaining more pride in a good golf swing rather than a hard one will pay dividends. |
| Chunking chips | Pokkie (Pace of play) | Make a deal with Pokkie. Tell him that you'll take half the time to set up for chip shots if he'll help you hit them better. Line them up, take your stance, say, "Here it goes, Pokkie," and hit away. | Chunking shots near the green upsets everybody, including your playing companions. Pokkie hates to see that and will rush in to help out. |
| Lack of distance | Susan (Accuracy) | Dress in your best golf clothes before you try to get her attention. Any less and your chances are about nil. Call softly and gently to her, making sure your playing companions know whom you are trying to reach. Tell her you want to loosen up and hit the big dog. | The golf gods can get bored with helping with the same old problems. Susan wouldn't mind some excitement. Helping someone go deep might be just what she needs sometimes. |

| | | | |
|---|---|---|---|
| Having a terrible day | Bacysos (Holes in one) | If the day is being caused by a disorganized committee or just bad golf, this will work. Listen to your inner self to hear Bacysos's words. Whatever comes to mind will be right—maybe not obvious, but right. | Let him know you are feeling miserable and need a swing thought to get you back on track. He'll come up with one of his sayings that will give you just what you need to refocus. |
| Topping the ball | Nogoeh (Protecting par) | Nogoeh is one of the most practical golf gods. He's also MacGyver-like in making tools out of junk. He can make your swing flaw into an asset. Just keep your praise light, simple, and natural. | Let Nogoeh know you are asking for his help. After that, before each swing, think of a majestic animal, a different one for each swing. Then hit away. Give him thanks at the end of each hole. |

You probably noticed that you can ask a golf god for help even if that god is not the obvious first choice. That's the point. They don't want rote; they want to develop a creative, evolving relationship with you. Feel free to ask any golf god for anything. Just be polite, be respectful, and accept responses you may not understand or agree with. They may sometimes ask that you do odd things. That's okay; do them.

Consider each request of a golf god to be like a first date. Be on your best behavior, listen to their every word, don't expect too much, don't go too fast, and do your best to just be yourself.

Unfortunately, we now have to take a look at the date from hell.

# Golf Demons
# (The Anti–Golf Gods)

The golf demons are nasty little devils. All three of them are inside us, and that's not just golfers. No, sir. Golf demons and all the other demons are in everyone, all the six billion and more people in the world, golfers and nongolfers, man and woman, boy and girl, young and old. All demons are in all of us. Golf demons are golf demons only because they seem to engorge themselves on golfing events just like other demons feast on politics, religion, sex, basketball, freeway driving, and so on. This demon infestation first occurred, of course, with Cain and Abel. In those ancient days it was a simple matter of good versus evil. There was one devil demon who prompted people to do bad things. This either/or system of good or bad worked pretty well for tens of thousands of years.

Slowly, over eons, demon specialties developed. This was obviously needed because humans became more complex. Life was no longer life or death, feast or famine, single or married. Life became mental health days from work, answering e-mails, screening phone calls, double-tall lattes, and pitching behind the batter. What was good behavior and what was bad behavior became lost in a fog of options. Only a specialist would know when it was truly bad to fudge on your taxes, forward a good-luck chain letter, or go forty in a thirty-five.

What happened a few thousand years ago was that first devil demon divided into what are now known as the seven deadly sins, then those seven further divided into the current demons—numbered at last count at 101,286. They all take up residence in your spleen. This is one of the reasons why it is so dangerous to rupture your spleen in a car accident—all the bad stuff gets loose, suddenly, rudely, and those demons are angry like a hive of hornets.

The demons don't multiply like humans. They are not male or female—they are "its." They create themselves by splitting from an existing demon and grow by absorbing other demons that aren't paying close enough attention and by ingesting the evil thoughts and deeds of humans.

Picture demons as maggots crawling over putrid garbage, except that the putrid garbage and the maggots are inside your body. Fortunately for us they're so small they're invisible. In fact, all of them take up no space at all. Physicists studying subatomic particles would have a field day studying demons since demons are a great example of energy without mass. In a way, they also don't have intention. This means they don't set off to do bad things. They don't decide, "Gee, I think I'll make that tall fellow in the green shirt trip that old lady with the cane." Simply put, they are pure evil with wide areas of influence to make a bad thing worse.

Luckily, only three demons have much to do specifically with golf. These were named earlier: Kcom, Orgo, and Minerv. These three are the only ones left of a whole slew of demons who were interested in golf but who were gobbled up by this ruthless trio. Demons don't actually have names. Basically, they have labels put on them by demonologists. These are people who spend their days and nights studying demons and talking about them, even writing books and creating web sites. They label the demons by what they seem to do most of. It's not like a golf god you can call on by name when you want something. Demons sense some potential for evil, then do what they can to enhance it.

Think of the demons as viruses in your body, ready to do harm at every opportunity. You will never get fully rid of them— as long as you're alive, anyway. The best you can do is restrict their access to your mind and heart, minimize their effect when loose, and make amends for whatever damage they caused as soon as the dust clears. The more you know about them, the better off you'll be. But in reality you will never be safe. They strike out of nowhere.

Your best bet is to be aware of what demons are operating in you and do your best to notice when they're trying to take charge. Demons cannot take over a person completely except for a few unfortunate souls, including two popular television evangelists, eleven Washington, D.C., politicians, two golfers currently playing on the American PGA Tour, and one on the European Tour. You always have a choice: to give in to their influence or overcome them with good character and a record of doing the right thing.

Read on to learn a bit about the three golf demons. It will not be pleasant. You might realize that you have been allowing them to take over sometimes. But be not afraid. The more you know about the demons, the better you can protect yourself and your loved ones.

# Kcom

### Area of Interest

Feeds primarily off your deepest wishes, fears, and thoughts

### Biography

Kcom is a direct descendent of both gluttony and greed and is distantly related to lust. None of the demons have actual names, of course. There is no need, since none talk to one another. "Kcom" is more like a designation, similar to the Los Angeles airport being LAX. Kcom got its most recent designation for helping invent radio commercials. Years later it helped in the creation of pop-ups on your computer. Any designation is used only until a greater misdeed is consummated, as when the demon of tooth decay managed to start World War II. Kcom is ready for a promotion, and it may come from golf.

Kcom's other designation almost 2,000 years ago was "Wyn," when one of his interests, wine, created a fuss. It was during a small house party given by Emperor Nero for a few of his friends. The party started off with some wine and cheese. Most guests chose a red from the central area of modern Italy. A minority chose a white from the German colony. The discussion about the relative merits of red over white or white over red led to a test, valid in those days, to determine which wine was superior.

Two slaves were called in to quickly down twenty-six goblets of wine; one drank white, the other red. The test was to see which slave would become intoxicated and die first. The better wine was the one that killed fastest.

Sensing this contest Demon Wyn accelerated the effect of the wine. As both slaves drank, the guests crowded in to see the results. Nero began to play popular drinking songs on his fiddle. Before you could say "bottoms up" in Latin, slave number two panicked and began screaming, and trying to break through the circle of spectators. Slave number one, believing the other slave was somehow cheating, began chasing him. The crowd stumbled back from the two slaves, knocking over the torches that lit the poolside where the party was being held. Drapes quickly caught fire, which immediately spread to the carpets and curtains in nearby rooms. Nero continued to play, eyes closed, as the fire spread across Rome.

### Effect on Golfer

The best way to understand what Kcom can do to a golfer is to imagine the worst decision you ever made on a course or the worst thing that ever happened to you on the course. Kcom was almost assuredly responsible.

Say you face a 150-yard carry over a pond. Kcom will know in an instant if you have even a fleeting thought that "I don't think I can make it." Every time you'll be pulling another ball out of your bag and hitting three.

Or say your opponent is facing a tough downhill ten-foot putt. For a split second you wish him ill. He'll sink it and take twenty dollars out of your wallet. That's Kcom again, using that brief thought against you.

*Artist's Portrayal of Kcom*

Kcom will crucify you for every negative thought, for every time you get discouraged, and every time you let up. Why do you think Tiger Woods is such a grinder? He knows that if he lets up for even a millisecond, his career is over. Kcom would have a field day the instant Tiger felt any sense of entitlement. With his talent, Tiger realizes he has to work five times as hard as everyone else just to keep Kcom at bay.

Unless you play strictly by the rules, and sometimes even when you do, Kcom will burrow into your deepest wishes and fears, causing a great deal of heartache.

### How to Appease Kcom

You can't. Golf demons have no intention, no needs, no thoughts, no compassion. What they have is direction, enhancing whatever stimulates them to make things worse.

### How to Minimize Kcom's Effect

Like all demons, Kcom senses when you have even the slightest not-so-nice thoughts or feelings deep inside you, where you hardly ever visit. This part of you is so deep, Sigmund Freud didn't even know it existed. It's ten times deeper in you than your id, that part of you that gets you into trouble with the opposite sex.

There is talk in the emerging medical specialty of Octodemonology that some substances make demons stronger demons, especially Kcom. These substances are carbohydrates (the recent drop in the handicap of average golfers was caused by the popularity of the Atkins diet—expect them to go up again soon—and in fact, you might be surprised to know that golf handicaps have no relation to equipment developments but do fluctuate with carbohydrate intake), blush wines, more than four daily cups of Starbucks coffee, canned peaches, sunblock rated over 50, and, surprisingly, carrying a dime, a quarter, and a penny in your right pocket (which has to do with some sort of electromagnetic effect). However, researchers are also finding evidence that a few things may weaken Kcom. These are: two ounces daily of single malt whisky from the island of Islay, speaking English with a Jamaican accent when your ball is in a bunker, conceding a short putt during the back nine you're sure your opponent would miss, listening to an intellectual book on tape on your way to the course, and arriving home within half an hour of the time you told your spouse you would be home. Current thinking is that some of these activities are so boring that Kcom is happy to go elsewhere for fun. Others are so thoughtful and good they may make Kcom sick. These findings are preliminary, however, and there are no guarantees.

The best thing that you can do is accept that some of your deep dark wishes and fears make you vulnerable to Kcom's influence. Do your best to be a strong individual and a good team player. Think of yourself *and* others.

# *Orgo*

## *Area of Interest*

Neglect

## *Biography*

Orgo is a direct descendant of Sloth and has hardly changed in more than ten thousand years. It is one of the purest demons. Of the three golf demons, Orgo is probably the strongest. In fact, of all the demons, Orgo is one of the most prevalent in affecting the welfare of mankind. When no one cares, evil is free to exploit every weakness in one person, a group, or even a nation.

Orgo was in full bloom in ancient Rome and in its glory during the days of the Inquisition. It was severely beaten back during the early twentieth century when many countries were attempting to create a truly free and unified world. It rebounded during World War II and later, when isolationist policies and self-serving actions by the more powerful nations reinvigorated Orgo to the strength it enjoys today.

## *Effect on Golfer*

This is a tough one. The fact is that every time you have a decision to make, unless you make a decision to take action, you're adding to its power. Even if your decision is a good one, like not attempting to hit a 3-wood over a canyon requiring a 255-yard carry, not doing something you thought about doing acts like a tonic to Orgo.

Any time you decide not to do something, Orgo gains strength. It doesn't seem fair. Actually, it isn't fair, but that's how it works with demons.

If you have a 7-iron in your hand and then decide not to use it, bam, Orgo is tuned in and turned on. Poor Colin Montgomery in the 2006 U.S. Open had a chance to win on the last hole. He was tied for the lead. A par would have won it for him. He was in the middle of the fairway, only a mid-iron from the green. He had a 6-iron in his hand. Unfortunately, he decided not to use

*Artist's Portrayal of Orgo*

it. To Orgo this meant Colin was neglecting his 6-iron. When Colin used his 7-iron (correctly thinking that his surge of adrenaline would give him extra power), Orgo made sure the ball fell short into deep grass and in a position impossible to hit from.

The same kind of thing has probably happened to you. You decided on a club, you changed your mind and tried to hit another. You may have been right, but Orgo made it bad. Good decision. Bad shot. But that's golf. Actually, that's Orgo.

### How to Appease Orgo

Can't be done. Worse, even the simple neglect of not informing someone that the toilet paper is out in a public bathroom energizes the little snot to a significant degree.

### How to Minimize Orgo's Effect

You can minimize Orgo's effect when playing golf by always playing offensively. Try not to play too aggressively; that won't work. Doing so would bring Obsissa into play. Consider golf to be a game of all offense and no defense, and you'll be mostly free of Orgo's always vigilant sense of neglect. Think through all your options before choosing your club, but don't take too long; otherwise, that's neglect. Fix ball marks. Rake traps. Hit balls before you play. Not doing so is a sign of neglecting your game.

Stick with your first instinct as much as you can. Read a putt quickly, then stand up and hit the ball. Strange as it may seem, miss quick and you'll miss less.

Whatever you do, don't neglect anything in your daily life. Too many people do, and that keeps Orgo grossly fat. Keep the air pressure in your tires at the right level. Visit your dentist regularly. Get that sigmoidoscopy and those mammograms when they're due. Visit your in-laws every fourth Sunday. Exercise three times a week, and shine your shoes every once in a while. Orgo will weaken, and the world will be a better place.

# *Minerv*

## Area of Interest

Dishonor

## Biography

You would think when Cain slew Abel that that would be the start of dishonor along with everything else. It wasn't, because the concept hadn't been invented yet. Evil was about it in those days for anything that was technically bad. Things were all or none. You were good or you were evil. You were going to heaven or you were going to hell. Things were easy then. You broke a promise to God and you were toast, literally and usually immediately.

It wasn't until many centuries later, when tens of thousands of people roamed the earth outside the Garden of Eden, that honor and thus dishonor came into being. It happened like this. Eight extended families lived in a small village called Uyela, smack in the middle of what is now the Sahara desert. In those days it was a fertile valley, full of game, water, vast tracts of farm land, and clean air. Life was rich and the people were thankful. This was a good place to be in those days.

One Saturday morning, Ona asked his neighbor Juso if he would help him repair his roof that day, and if so they would work together on Juso's roof the next Saturday. Juso thought this was fine and they shook hands, a new gesture replacing the ancient bonking of foreheads. They labored together all day in the hot sun to repair Ona's roof. Alas, on the next Saturday Ona failed to show up at Juso's house. When asked later that afternoon what happened, Ona replied, "I just didn't feel like helping you. I wanted to rest in the shade. In fact, I'm not going to help you repair your roof at all. Do it yourself." Aghast, Juso didn't know what to think. What his neighbor did wasn't evil, but it sure wasn't nice. Juso muttered to himself all day wondering how to fathom what his neighbor had done.

At dinner that night he told his wife, "I'm going into the village this evening and diss Ona."

"What?"

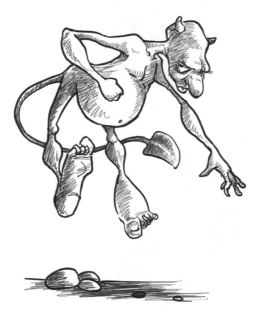

*Artist's Portrayal of Minerv*

"I'm going to diss Ona," he said again. "Diss Ona. He did a very bad thing. So it's diss Ona from now on." And so it has been, and also, thus Minerv was born.

### Effect on Golfer

There isn't much that needs be said about dishonor because there is so much of it. Young and inexperienced golfers do it to the game all the time. A nine on the course becomes a seven on the card almost automatically. This is because the young and inexperienced have not yet made a commitment to golf's code of honor. In fact, it does golfers honor that they even have a code of honor. Most games, and all those "officiated" in one way or another by umpires, referees, and judges, promote getting away with all you can. If the ref didn't see it, it didn't happen. Imagine a society operating like that.

Anyway, Minerv has been quite content for the last hundred thousand years or so, feeding off individual acts of selfishness in most games and most life activities, except golf. That's what has created such a huge problem.

Minerv looks to golfers to feed its power, for when a golfer commits a dishonor, Minerv's influence expands like your waistline at Thanksgiving. Claim a five handicap when you're a nine, Minerv wins. Claim a twenty when you're a ten, Minerv wins. Give yourself a putt of more than twenty inches, Minerv wins.

When you go against golf's honor code, Minerv wins. When you do the right thing, Minerv tries to make things worse. With its accumulated power, if you do what's honorable and call a penalty on yourself, Minerv will do its best to ensure it will cost you money if not the match and a championship trophy. Minerv was the actual originator of the saying, "No good deed goes unpunished."

Bob Jones almost eliminated Minerv when he declared that you may as well praise a man for not robbing a bank when someone commented on his honesty. However, when Ty Cobb and a few others took up golf with a win-at-any-cost attitude, Minerv had new life.

Minerv will test your nerve and your commitment to golf's core values. Minerv will watch for every opportunity you have to make a dishonorable decision on the course. If only half your decisions are honorable, it gains power. If ninety percent are honorable, it's a draw. If every one is honorable, you've contributed to the betterment of all mankind and chopped a piece out of Minerv.

### How to Appease Minerv

Again, no can do. Few of us look out for the other guy before we think of ourselves. A few saints are born every now and then who do that but for the rest of us, it's "what's in it for me?" Minerv has thrived off of this attitude from the days of Babylonia.

You can see this anytime, anywhere. Drive on any street or highway at the speed limit. What you're doing, driving at the speed limit, is driving safely according to the engineers who built the road and those who monitor traffic on that road. You're driving safely for you and everyone else. How many people whiz by you? Everyone, right? What are they thinking? They're thinking screw the speed limit, I have to get where I'm going as soon as I can or it will be just awful. There is no thought for anyone else. Get the picture? As long as we think we're the center of the universe it fosters the nesting of more maggots in your spleen than you could ever imagine.

Minerv has gained influence over you if you knowingly break a rule and don't admit it. Minerv has gained control over you if, off the course, you consider that life rules (like brushing your teeth twice a day, returning rental DVDs on time, and waiting your turn) are for chumps, not for special people like you.

### How to Minimize Minerv's Effect

Once you have some idea how to play golf, honor the core values of honesty, integrity, and playing the ball and course as you find them, and contribute to the game when you play. Become a steward of golf.

Do the same in life. Believe that you are part of something big—humanity—and contribute. Do your share and just a bit more. Can you imagine living in a place where everyone did that? And since this isn't happening now, can you imagine your contribution to a better world if you did your share and a bit more, and encouraged others to do the same?

Embrace golf's values, and do likewise in your daily life. Join Keepers of the Game and invite your friends. In one generation Minerv could be eliminated.

# Some Golfers' Thoughts About the Golf Gods

Comments from many golfers, from many walks of life, have been collected to help you better understand how the golfing community embraces or doesn't embrace the golf gods. It's useful to note that different types of golfers relate differently to the golf gods. Professional golfers, for example, will try anything and do almost anything in the search for lower scores. Believing in the golf gods is an easy thing to do for a win or top finish. It's even easier when you realize that professional golfers are prisoners of superstition. Dave Pelz has made a career out of understanding golf shots through scientific analysis. His findings confirmed that for chips from off the green, leaving the flagstick in increases the chances of the ball going in the hole. But watch tour players. Many pull the flag out for these chips. Why would they do that if it actually lessens the probability of making the shot? To them, it "feels" like the right thing to do. Thus, many "feel" like they should believe in the golf gods. Like Pascal's wager, it can't hurt.

Amateur golfers are even less discriminating in their quest for improvement. Dozens of inventors have made fortunes selling one golf improvement gimmick after another to a crowd thirsty for any sip at the cup of success. Believing in the golf gods is a no-brainer.

These facts, of course, explain why the golf gods wanted this book to be published. The golf gods are not needy. They are not desperate to be worshipped by the greedy or the brainwashed masses. They want a partnership with you, a way for both golf gods and mortals to embrace and enjoy the best of games.

The following comments have been derived from many sources: from the golf gods themselves, the World Wide Web, traditionally published sources, personal contact, and channeling from three highly regarded channelers, Soppopo from

Greece, Jeth from Wisconsin, and Rimanchik from a small, unnamed Peruvian village in the Andes.

Read them to get a feel for how others understand the golf gods. Then think about what comments you would make if you were asked. The golf gods are interested in what you would say— and will enjoy listening to your opinions. As you have learned, state the name of the golf god you want to talk to, say what you have to say out loud, and rest assured that you will be heard.

### Cameron Morfit, Senior Writer, GOLFONLINE

*Granted, the Golf Gods exist, there's no argument about that. And it only follows that the Golf Gods' world headquarters (GGHQ) is Over There, across "the pond," in the United Kingdom.*

### Michelle Wie, Famous female golfer

*In a tournament once I chunked a chip in front of a lot of people. After I finished the hole I stomped toward the next tee. There was a gallery rope there, and I tripped on it and cut my leg. I still have the scar. It was the golf gods getting even with me. If you expect a bad lie even for one second, the gods will know it and give you a bad lie because you deserve it for thinking that way.*

### Ruth Valzenso, Weekend golfer from Two Rivers, Iowa

*I've played golf for over thirty years. Someone mentioned the golf gods to me about ten years ago, and I said it was a bunch of hooey. I've been playing worse since then because of my arthritis. It is certainly not anything to do with them. I was a 12 handicap and now I'm a 35. I'll get my game back. The steep decline in my game has nothing to do with them. Nothing at all.*

### United States Golf Association, Executive Committee

#### Channeled by Soppopo

*We are well aware of the golf gods, of course. In spite of that knowledge, it is our new contention that play-offs do not need the equalizer of well-formed golf god committees. More specifically, we are referring to eighteen-hole play-offs for our prestigious national titles. We believe every player has had the benefit of four committees though the four rounds of the championship, and the level of functioning of any new committee formed for any length play-off we will consider "rub-of-the-green." For that reason we are seriously considering going to a multi-hole play-off system like the British Open. We will seek the golf gods' comments, however, before we finalize our decision.*

### Annika Sorenstam, Professional golfer

#### Channeled by Jeth

*I saw one once. I said "hello." The next day I shot the first 59 on the LPGA tour. I believe in the golf gods, and I will always believe. (Do you hear that, Umuligt?)*

### Mrs. Bob Murphy, Wife of Tour Pro

*In the mid 70s Bob was struggling with his putting (as he has off and on in his career), but everyone that looked at him said his stroke looked absolutely fine, as did his tempo. But nothing would go in the hole. His dad's next younger brother, Father Jerome Murphy, was a Redemptorist priest at a mission in the jungle in Brazil. There they had carved a golf course out of the jungle, which they played as often as they could. Father Jerome used to write Bob at least once a month on tour and let him know they were all watching his scores, and then either congratulate him on the good rounds or counsel him on just what they thought (in their humble opinions) was wrong with his game. After struggling with the putting for a while, Bob wrote Father Jerome and asked him to say a few prayers to the "Golf God" to help his putting improve. Bob told Father Jerome that as far as he was concerned, the "God of Golf" was dead because he couldn't make a three-footer. After a week or so we heard back from Jerome, and he informed us that the "God of Golf" was alive and well in the jungles of Brazil. He was putting the best he ever had and thought they would keep him in Brazil for a while longer. Bob would have to work on his putting by himself.*

### Malcolm Ferrier, Chairman, Keepers of the Game

*I'm quite sure a golf god lived in a tree between the seventh and the eleventh greens on my local course. It perched there to help wayward shots somehow manage to miss the deep and dreaded glen that was all too nearby. The chances of hitting the tree and going into the glen were, I suppose, pretty close to 50/50. But the ball seldom did—in fact it would quite often find its way to the edge of the green. No other way else to*

202 &#x211E; *The Golf Gods*

*explain this except to recognize and acknowledge the golf god that surely made this happen. A belated thank-you, Sir or Madam!*

## Ozzy Osbourne, Rocker

### Channeled by Jeth

*The golf gods are \*&%$)\* which really @!$&^%. I think they are #$@\*&%)> and that goes for golfers too.*

## Arnold Palmer, Professional golfer

### Channeled by Rimanchik

*I must thank the golf gods for some of my skill and good fortune. My father Deacon believed in them. He would make the golf gods peanut butter-and-jelly sandwiches, slice off the crust and cut them into little squares, and leave them on a green in the evening. They were always gone the next day. We didn't know what they liked in those days, but I guess they really liked those sandwiches. Actually, we knew it was probably squirrels that took those sandwiches, but it was fun to imagine the golf gods enjoying them. They have certainly blessed my life, and I am happy giving back to golf and the golf gods whatever I can. I suppose I would like being a golf god, but not any time soon.*

## Dave Pelz, Golf Scientologist

### Channeled by Jeth

*They don't exist. I can't prove they don't exist yet, but I will.*

## Ben Hogan, Professional golfer

### Channeled by Soppopo

*Most people understand that I worked very hard to achieve consistency with my golf swing. I also created a golf club company that refused to offer the public anything less than the best. However, I want to confess that much of my moral compass was derived by personal coaching from Masfel, without whom I would have been lost.*

## The Golf Grouch, Golfer who loves the game

*My love for the game of golf was completely reinvigorated by the mercy of the golf gods. As Michael Corleone said in* The Godfather,

Part III, *"Just when I thought I was out, they pull me back in." Yes, Michael, "they" are the golf gods.*

## Tiger Woods, Professional golfer

### Channeled by Rimanchik

*I believe in the golf gods the same way I believe in establishing goals and having strong values. It's all about perspective. I've been fortunate to be able to understand what needs to be done and why it should be done, and I am often able to find a way to get it done. Life is a series of events, and each one needs to be understood separately. All you have are the moments, so make the most of them. One shot at a time. As Foot the caddie once told me, "A bad shot is only as bad as the next shot makes it." The idea is to make the current shot a good one no matter what happened before. Now is all that you have and all that counts. If I were to become a golf god, I think I'd like to be the golf god of seizing the moment.*

## Jim Corbett, "Mr. Golf Etiquette"

*Albert Einstein once said, "God does not play dice with the universe." But I play golf with Albert Finkelstein, and he once chili-dipped a wedge shot over a lake only to have it skip off the back of a turtle, bounce off the beverage cart, take three bounding leaps down the cart path, roll across the green, and go straight into the cup. So I say, "Physics, schmizics." The golf gods are definitely playing golf with the universe. Why do you think the stars and planets are round? What else could be the purpose of a Black Hole?*

## William Howard Taft, Twenty-seventh U.S. President

*William McKinley may have been the first United States President to play golf, but I promoted this great game from the White House long before Old Ike entered the picture. I was aware of the golf gods and often sought their counsel. There were only fourteen of them in my day (1909). Here is my thought. For success in troubled times consult with the golf gods, for they will always light the way for any good purpose.*

## Jack Nicklaus, Professional golfer

### Channeled by Soppopo

*I'm aware that one of my nicknames during my tour days was "Carnac" (The Magician, a Johnny Carson character), because I always seemed to think I knew everything. Usually I did know everything. Not a week went by without Phor or other golf gods contacting me about one problem or another. I helped him and the others as well as I could while still saving enough time to play on the tour and be a good father and husband. It took a lot of time and energy to help out all the golf gods. I can't imagine how many more majors I would have won without this added burden.*

## Oprah Winfrey, Talk show hostess

### Channeled by Soppopo

*I don't play golf, I've played miniature golf some, which is totally boring, but Steadman has played on a real golf course. I love the idea of a golf god for new women golfers. Women need that support. Some people say I have a bias toward women, and that I support them and promote them more than I do men. That is true, but not because of weakness, but of need, something entirely different. I am trying to enable women to take our rightful place in the development of our world. I plan to have Sarah Winston on my show as soon as possible, and we women are going to rock.*

## Mark Huber, PGA caddie

*I've been a professional caddie for eighteen years, and I feel their presence during every round. If I start to walk away from a fresh divot, I feel something pulling me back to make sure every effort is made to repair the blemish. Nine times out of ten if I don't respond properly there will be a lipped-out putt or the dreaded 3-putt waiting at the green. A coincidence or the "Golf Gods?"*

*During shot selection there are usually three or four choices but only one right decision. If that right decision isn't made, the consequences can be disastrous. During my discussion with the pro, I can usually sense someone or something leading me toward the right decision. If I don't follow this lead we usually add a shot or two to our score. Are the "Golf Gods" present, and punishing us for that bad choice?*

*Raymond Floyd won his last tournament at the 2000 Ford Senior Championship. It was a major, and I was beside him on the bag. We were tied for the lead, our tee ball on the eighteenth hole had found the rough, and we were faced with a difficult decision. As Raymond caressed the two irons he was thinking about, he turned to me and said,*

*"Come on, feel this shot; we both have to feel it; feel the shot with me."*
*At that point a tremendous calm gathered over me and all I could see*
*was the perfect shot leaving Raymond's clubface.*

*Watching Raymond's hand slide to the club, I was also thinking*
*about how there seemed to be some sort of transference between the*
*two of us without anything being spoken. He struck the perfect shot,*
*handed me the club, and smiled. We walked to the green; he made the*
*putt, and won the tournament. Nothing else was present, not the crowd,*
*not the emotions; nothing was in focus except the shot. Where did that*
*calm come from, considering that I was extremely nervous just seconds*
*before? Were the "Golf Gods" there by my side?*

*All I know is that there are right and wrong things to do on the golf*
*course every step of the way. The decisions we make have an outcome on*
*our score and the game of golf. I believe the consequences of our decisions*
*are judged and dealt out by something or someone other than the "rub*
*of the green."*

You can see that some golfers believe in the golf gods and
some don't. In the grand scheme of things, this is okay. The golf
gods hope that those who believe will now know how to inter-
act with the golf gods to everyone's satisfaction. They also hope
that some disbelievers will change their minds.

Even so, for staunch nonbelievers, there is still hope.

# The Final Word

All of the world's religions face the same reality: there are more people who disbelieve in any particular religion than believe. Religions handle this fact in varied ways. A few send people door to door to win souls. Others at some time in their histories have tried to make converts by bonking nonbelievers over the head.

Although not part of a religion, the golf gods face the same problem. More golfers don't believe in the golf gods than do believe. If, after reading this golf gods book, you are still a disbeliever, you are not doomed to golf purgatory. You can benefit from knowing about the golf gods even if you believe they don't exist.

There is a subtle psychological model called the "lessening effect." It is part of what psychologists call "superstitious behavior," part of what they call "locus of control," part of what they call "power of suggestion," part of what they call "self-fulfilling prophecy," part of what they call "self-efficacy," part of what they call "affirmations," part of what they call "displacement," and part of about seven other esoteric psychological concepts. All in all it is something well known to them and completely unknown to the rest of us. Some of them call it the "Stone Effect," after W. Clement Stone, who once wrote, "Whatever the mind of man can conceive and believe, it can achieve." In this case, the lessening effect lessens the affect of outside influences, namely the golf gods.

Here is how the lessening effect or the Stone Effect actually works. If you say to someone who is biting into an apple, "That apple is sour," they will taste sourness. The apple is perfectly fine, but your statement that it wasn't affects the other person's perception. However, according to the lessening effect, if the person rejects your statement about the apple being sour the apple will actually taste sweet. This would be the case even if the person knew nothing about the lessening effect, but the effect is stronger if you know about it.

This is how things work to your advantage with the golf gods. If someone mentions the golf gods and you truly believe that's really stupid, through the lessening effect you have just given your self-esteem a boost and enhanced your sense of control over your golf game, which directly increases your ability to hit the ball.

Last fall researchers at the University of Hawaii conducted an experiment to see if the lessening effect actually worked with golfers in regard to belief or disbelief in the golf gods. For the entire month of November they tested every fifth golfer who played on the resort courses of Maui and Kauai. They took the golfer aside and asked him/her about the golf gods. They divided the responders into three groups, active believers, those who were strongly against the existence of the golf gods, and those who were neutral. Through some pretty sophisticated statistical analysis they determined that believers scored best and enjoyed the round the most, nonbelievers who were asked about the golf gods and disavowed them were second, and the neutral (control) group was last; these were statistically significant differences.

What this means for you, as a nonbeliever, is this: if you want to benefit from the lessening effect and play better golf, all you have to do before a round of golf is rant and rave about the nonexistence of the golf gods. The lessening effect will be even stronger if you said to your playing companions, "You know, the whole idea of golf gods is totally bogus." If they really don't exist, it's a scientific fact you'll play better than you normally would — that is, *if* they don't exist.

# Post-Final Word

Assuming that the golf gods exist, a new awareness will permeate your game as you and the golf gods become friends. You'll enjoy golf as never before. It should be clear by now, however, that the golf gods will not perform magic tricks with your ball. They won't answer calls to make your ball fly through solid objects or dip and swoop through the air like a barn swallow, although, of course, they could if they wanted to.

This is a typical story of a golf god and a golfer.

George Hewitt had asked Wooda one season to be his guardian golf god. George made that decision out of desperation. His first-tee jitters were so bad he could hardly keep the ball on the tee and certainly couldn't put a good swing on it. Invariably his round was ruined either by total humiliation on the tee or a horrendous score on the first hole of the day.

Once he asked Wooda to help out, George dutifully wrote Wooda's name on his scorecard each time he played, drew a smiley face with ears, tugged on his own ear just before taking his first swing of the day, and even played jazz on his way to the course. He was rewarded with an absence of tension on the first tee all summer.

The last tournament of the year at his club was the annual member-guest. George had grown confident enough to invite his boss. George was up for promotion and figured a great game with his boss would help his chances.

He worried, though, about his first-tee jitters returning and asked Wooda "to make sure the day turned out well."

On the day of the tournament, George was confident on the first tee. He graciously invited his boss to hit first. Mr. Crump hit a beauty down the middle. It was George's turn.

He felt great reaching for his club. He felt great walking to the tee box. He felt great sticking his tee into the ground. Unfortunately, as he was about to place his ball on the tee, panic paralyzed every muscle in his body. He couldn't move. He couldn't breathe.

He also couldn't get the ball to stay on the tee. His heart pounded. His hands shook so much they knocked it off ten times in a row. Finally the ball was balanced on the tee.

He took his stance, addressed the ball with his driver, and accidentally pushed the ball off the tee. Ten more attempts with trembling hands were needed to get the ball to stay on the tee again.

Wiser this time, he stood at the ball and quickly swung, and missed. He swung again and missed again. Taking a deep breath George steadied himself and swung once more. The ball sailed out of bounds to the right.

"That's okay, George," his boss said. "It's a better ball tournament, and maybe I can do well with mine."

George was crushed. He was angry at Wooda. How could his guardian golf god let him down at such an important moment?

George collected himself and played decent golf over the remaining seventeen holes. He and Mr. Crump had a pretty good time. As they were walking off the eighteenth green, Mr. Crump brought up the first tee. "You know, George," he said. "That was a shame on the first tee. I could see how nervous you were. I guess that's to be expected playing with your boss and all. What I didn't expect was to see how well you handled yourself afterward. That was good. Come by my office next week and let's talk about that promotion of yours."

At that point George realized that Wooda had been helping in just the right way. Unbeknownst to George, Wooda had even enlisted the aid of Otom and Masfel to ensure success. Golf gods are like that. Have a great time with your new friends.

To contact the golf gods:
golfgods.info